THE TRIALS
GREAT BIBLE
CHARACTERS

Clarence E. Macartney

Books by Clarence E. Macartney

Chariots of Fire
The Faith Once Delivered
Great Characters of the Bible
Great Interviews of Jesus
Great Women of the Bible
The Greatest Questions of the Bible and of Life
The Greatest Texts of the Bible
The Greatest Words of the Bible and in Human Speech
He Chose Twelve
The Parables of the Old Testament
Parallel Lives of the Old and New Testaments
Paul the Man
The Prayers of the Old Testament
Strange Texts but Grand Truths
Trials of Great Bible Characters
Twelve Great Questions About Christ
The Wisest Fool: Sermons on Bible Characters

THE TRIALS OF GREAT BIBLE CHARACTERS

Clarence E. Macartney

kregel
PUBLICATIONS

Grand Rapids, MI 49501

Until life's trial time shall end,
And heavenly peace be won.
—William J. Irons

The Trials of Great Bible Characters by Clarence E. Macartney

Published in 1996 by Kregel Publications, a division of Kregel, Inc., P.O. Box 2607, Grand Rapids, MI 49501. Kregel Publications provides trusted, biblical publications for Christian growth and service. Your comments and suggestions are valued.

Cover photograph: Copyright © 1996, Kregel, Inc.
Cover and book design: Alan G. Hartman

Library of Congress Cataloging-in-Publication Data
Macartney, Clarence Edward Noble, 1879–1957
    The trials of great Bible characters / Clarence E. Macartney.
        p.   cm.
    Originally published: New York; Nashville: Abingdon-Cokesbury Press, 1946.
    1. Bible—Biography—Sermons. 2. Sermons, American.
3. Presbyterian Church—Sermons. I. Title.
BS571.5.M37   1996   252'.051—dc20   96–11435
                                                                    CIP

ISBN 0-8254-3285-5

1 2 3 4 5 Printing / Year 00 99 98 97 96

CONTENTS

Foreword 6

1. The Trial of Job 8
2. The Trial of Abraham 18
3. The Trial of Jacob 25
4. The Trial of Joseph 33
5. The Trial of Moses 42
6. The Trial of David 50
7. The Trial of Elijah 58
8. The Trial of Daniel 68
9. The Trial of Ezekiel 77
10. The Trial of Peter 86
11. The First Trial of Jesus 96
12. The Trial of John Mark 106
13. The Trial of Judas 114
14. The Trial of Paul 125
15. The Last Trial of Jesus 135

FOREWORD

In these sermons it will be seen that I have used the word "trial" in its broad and scriptural meaning, that is, as a test. Sometimes the trial, or test, to which the men discussed were subjected was in the nature of a temptation to evil, as in the case of Joseph and Judas. Sometimes the trial was a matter of conscience, as in the case of Daniel. Quite often the trial was something painful and hard which tested the faith of those who were tried. We see that kind of trial in the life of Abraham, in the life of Ezekiel, in the sufferings of Job, in Paul's thorn in the flesh, and in the last trial of our Lord, when He drew back for a moment from His cup in the Garden of Gethsemane.

The preachers of a former day frequently used the word "probation." It is unfortunate that the word itself—and too often the idea back of it—has dropped out of the language of the preacher today. Life is indeed a trial, a probation, the purpose of which is to test us, to see what is in our heart, to develop moral and spiritual qualities within us, with a view to their complete unfolding and coronation in the life to come.

The reaction to these messages on the part of men and women who themselves were passing through sore trials has prompted me to send the sermons forth in this more permanent form, with the hope and prayer that they will bring strength and comfort to others in such circumstances.

The preacher who preaches on this subject has a double advantage. In the first place, he is dealing with the lives of the great personalities of the Scriptures, and when he is doing that, he is always coming close to the lives of men and women today. In the second place, what he says may be used of God to strengthen and sustain those who are in trouble.

CLARENCE EDWARD MACARTNEY

1

THE TRIAL OF JOB

When he hath tried me, I shall come forth as gold (Job 23:10).

The three great trials of the Bible are: First, the trial of Christ, who in Gethsemane, while He sweat as it were great drops of blood, prayed, "If it be possible, let this cup pass from me," and who on the cross cried out at the ninth hour, "My God, why hast thou forsaken me?" Second, the trial of Abraham, who was commanded to offer up Isaac on Mount Moriah. Third, the trial of Job, who was delivered into the hand of Satan.

Every man ought to read at least one great book before he dies. If you have read the book of Job, you have read the greatest of books. Here is a vastness and sublimity like that of the ocean, sometimes raging and mounting up to heaven, sometimes sleeping in infinite peace and resignation. Here we have intense sorrow and suffering, soul-searching interrogation, infinitely tender appeal, sublime faith in God, and Christlike trust and submission. The majesty of the book is due in part to the metaphors and similes. "Man is born unto trouble, as the sparks fly upward." The war horse "paweth in the valley," his neck "clothed with thunder." Job recalls his prosperous days "when I washed my steps with butter." The Lord asks out of the whirlwind, "Who shut up the sea with doors?" But the chief distinction of the book is not in its style but in its great treatment of a great theme, the sufferings of the righteous.

When did Job live? No one knows. Where was the land of Uz? No one is certain. Of what race or nationality was Job? We cannot be sure. All this is to our advantage, for Job stands out, not as a man of any particular race or age or land, but as universal man, facing life and grappling with suffering, destiny, and God. Suffering is the great problem of theology. It is the universal problem, as eternal as human history and as universal as human nature. It is to this problem of pain and suffering that not only theologians and philosophers address themselves, but government and science as well.

"There was a man in the land of Uz, whose name was Job; and that man was perfect and upright, and one that feared God, and eschewed evil." There is none perfect but God; and when it is said here of Job that he was perfect, no doubt what is meant is that the whole tenor of his life was Godward. Job had seven sons and three daughters. His flocks and herds cast their shadows upon a thousand hills, for his substance was "seven thousand sheep, and three thousand camels, and five hundred yoke of oxen, and five hundred she asses, and a very great household." Job was the greatest, the richest, man of all the East, and his piety was in proportion to his prosperity. John prayed for his friend Gaius, "that thou mayest prosper and be in health, even as thy soul prospereth." There are not a few who have worldly prosperity but whose spiritual prosperity is far behind their material possessions. But Job was a godly man. At his altar prayer never ceased, and every morning he made intercession for his sons and offered up sacrifices on their behalf.

"Now there was a day when the sons of God came to present themselves before the Lord, and Satan came also among them. And the Lord said unto Satan, 'Whence comest thou?' Then Satan answered the Lord, and said, 'From going to and fro in the earth, and from walking up and down in it.' And the Lord said unto Satan, 'Hast thou considered my servant Job, that there is none like him in the earth, a perfect and an upright man, one that feareth God, and escheweth evil?'" With a malignant sneer Satan answered, "Doth Job fear God for nought? Hast not thou made an hedge about him, and about his house, and . . . blessed the work of his hands . . . ? But put forth thine hand now, and touch all that he hath"—break down the hedge You have built about him—"and he will curse thee to thy face."

God accepted the challenge of Satan as to the disinterestedness of Job's piety, and Job was subjected in quick succession to four terrific trials: the loss of property, the loss of his loved ones, the loss of his health, and the loss of his reputation and good name. The pre-eminence of Job is that he was chosen by God to show to the world that there was at least one man who would serve God for nothing.

THE FIRST THREE TRIALS OF JOB

1. *The Loss of Property*—There came one day a messenger running to Job with news that, while the oxen were plowing in the field and the asses feeding beside them, a band of Sabeans had fallen on them, slain the servants, and run off the animals. Possibly, Job said when he heard this news, "This is a serious loss, but I still have left seven thousand sheep and three thousand camels." But the words were hardly out of his mouth before a second messenger came running and said to him, "The fire of God is fallen from heaven, and hath burned up the sheep, and the servants, and consumed them; and I only am escaped alone to tell thee." When he heard that, Job probably said, "Seven thousand sheep is a heavy loss to bear, but I still have left three thousand camels. I can sell some of the camels and replace some of the sheep and oxen which have been lost." But again, before the words were out of his mouth, a third messenger came running to tell him that three bands of Chaldeans had swooped down out of the desert, had slain the drivers with the edge of the sword, and had run off all the camels. That meant that all Job's earthly possessions were gone, gone in a single day! But under this trial Job did not curse God, as Satan had predicted, but said with noble resignation, "Naked came I out of my mother's womb, and naked shall I return thither." He echoed the as yet unspoken words of the Apostle Paul, "We brought nothing into this world, and it is certain we can carry nothing out."

2. *The Loss of Family and Loved Ones*—Job had nobly sustained the loss of his property, but a more severe trial awaited him. A man may be rich in this world's goods, but if he have none to love and be loved by, he is a pauper; whereas a man may lose all his property and yet be rich if he have those whom he loves and who love him. Perhaps after he had lost all his property Job said to himself, "I still have seven loyal and devoted sons and three affectionate daughters. They will care for me now, and give me a new start in life." But if so, that hope was shattered by the news which was brought to him by a fourth messenger. This one told him that as his sons and daughters were eating and drinking wine in the home of their eldest brother, a whirlwind "smote the four corners of the house," and it fell upon his children, and they were dead. But still Job did not curse God. In his great grief he "rent his mantle, and shaved his head, and fell down upon the ground, and worshiped, and said, . . . 'The Lord gave, and the Lord hath taken away; blessed be the name of the Lord.'" Job has stood the second great trial without faltering. Now comes the third trial.

3. *The Loss of Health*—There is a second conclave in heaven. "And the Lord said unto Satan, 'Hast thou considered my servant Job, . . . one that feareth God, and escheweth evil? and still he holdeth fast to his integrity, although thou movedst me against him, to destroy him without cause.'" Disdainfully Satan answers, "Skin for skin, yea, all that a man hath will he give for his life. But put forth thine hand now, and touch his bone and his flesh, and he will curse thee to thy face." God accepts this second challenge of Satan and permits Satan to smite Job in his body, but with this limitation: "He is in thine hand; but save his life." This limitation, as we shall see, constituted the sorest part of Job's trial. If only he had been permitted to die, he would have had no complaints. It was his prolonged suffering that troubled him. The increase in the intensity of his sufferings suggest that as strength and purity of character grow the severity of trial increases. This throws light on Paul's mysterious saying that "whom the Lord loveth he chasteneth."

Job was smitten with a loathsome disease, "sore boils from the sole of his foot unto his crown." Removing himself from his home, he sat down among the ashes and scraped himself with a potsherd. Then his wife spoke with him. One can hardly be sure whether she was moved by scorn or by pity for Job. But what she said to him was this: "Dost thou still retain thine integrity? curse God and die." To that Job rendered his sublime answer: "What? shall we receive good at the hand of God, and shall we not receive evil?" So "in all this did not Job sin with his lips." Job has withstood the third trial, the severe trial of bodily sickness, without flinching, holding fast to God.

At the end of these three trials—the loss of property, the loss of family, and the loss of health—Job has proved that he does serve God for nothing. He has proved that God is dearer to him than all else. He can now say these words of the hymn ascribed to Francis Xavier:

> My God, I love thee; not because
>   I hope for heaven thereby,
> Not yet because who love thee not
>   Must die eternally.
> Not with the hope of gaining aught,
>   Not seeking a reward;
> But as thyself hast loved me,
>   O ever-loving Lord!

THE FOURTH TRIAL

The fourth trial, the loss of his reputation and good name among his friends, is the sorest trial of all. Job had three old friends—Eliphaz the Temanite, Bildad the Shuhite, and Zophar the Naamathite. The grapevine of the desert had brought them the tidings of Job's trouble; and, making an appointment, they came from afar to mourn with Job and to comfort him. When they saw Job sitting there on the ash heap, scraping himself with a potsherd, at first they did not know him. They could not recognize him as the great emir whom they had known in the days of his prosperity. When Naomi came back from Moab with her daughter-in-law Ruth, her hair white and her face lined from the afflictions through which she had passed, her old neighbors in Bethlehem could hardly recognize her as the comely young matron who had left with her husband and her two sons some years before. As they gathered about her, they exclaimed one to another, "Is this Naomi?" So it was with the friends of Job as they said one to another, "Can this be Job?" For seven days they sat in eloquent silence and sympathy alongside of Job on his ash heap, but spoke not a word, "for they saw that his grief was very great." They were, as we shall see, oftentimes wrong in their theology; but they were beautifully right, at least at first, in their sympathy, in the theology of the heart, for they were touched with a feeling for Job's infirmities.

At length Job broke the silence and cursed the day he was born. "Let the day perish wherein I was born, and the night in which it was said, 'There is a man child conceived. . . . Let darkness and the shadow of death stain it. . . . Why died I not from the womb? . . . For now should I have lain still and been quiet. There the wicked cease from troubling; and there the weary be at rest.'"

Job did not curse God, but in cursing the day of his birth he came close to questioning the providence of God in his life. So at least it strikes his three friends. They now begin to speak with Job, each one in his turn, and Job answers. The first speaker, Eliphaz, commences with great courtesy and dignity, "If we assay to commune with thee, wilt thou be grieved?" At first the three friends of Job go no further than to exhort him to be strong and to trust in God. They express a mild surprise that Job, so renowned for his piety and for the comfort that he has given others, has no medicine now for himself. "Behold," they say, "thou hast instructed many, and thou hast strengthened the weak hands. Thy words have upholden him that was falling, and thou hast strengthened the feeble knees. But now it is come upon thee, and thou faintest; it toucheth thee, and thou art troubled."

To this they add the general proposition that God does not permit the innocent to perish: "Remember, I pray thee, who ever perished, being innocent? or where were the righteous cut off?" In this there is both hope and warning for Job—hope for him if he is innocent, but a warning to him that he must not lift himself up against the providence of God. This is declared by Eliphaz in one of the most thrilling passages of the whole debate, when he relates a vision of the night: "In thoughts from the visions of the night, when deep sleep falleth on men, fear came upon me, and trembling, which made all my bones to shake. Then a spirit passed before my face; the hair of my flesh stood up: . . . an image was before mine eyes, there was silence, and I heard a voice, saying, 'Shall mortal man be more just than God? shall a man be more pure than his maker?'" Having thus warned Job not to claim righteousness in the sight of God, they remind him that trouble is a part of human life and that "man is born unto trouble, as the sparks fly upward." The wise thing is not to question God's way, but to trust Him—"Happy is the man whom God correcteth: therefore despise not thou the chastening of the Almighty." If Job does as they advise him to do, and humbles himself before God, all will be well with him in the end. "Thou shalt come to thy grave in a full age, like a shock of corn cometh in his season."

But as Job continues to express his amazement, his three friends, who have come to comfort him, heated now by argument and debate, accuse Job of unworthiness. First they do it in a general and hypothetical way. Where there is great suffering, there must be great iniquity. Job must be a hypocrite in his former reputation for piety and in his present asseverations of innocence, and they pointedly remind him that the hope of hypocrites shall perish. Then they come out openly and charge Job with specific transgressions. He has taken a pledge from his brothers for nothing. He has stripped the naked, refused water to the weary, withdrawn bread from the hungry, sent widows away empty, and broken the arms of the fatherless. It is because he is a greater sinner than all men that these judgments have come upon him.

Sometimes with indignation, sometimes with pathetic appeal, Job denies these charges. He says that if he had been guilty of them, if he had walked with vanity, if he had been deceived by a woman, if he had caused the eyes of the widow to fail, if he had selfishly eaten his morsel alone, if he had seen any perish for want of clothing, or had made gold his hope, then he could understand why he suffered. He longs for vindication:

"Oh that I knew where I might find him! . . . Behold, I go forward, but he is not there; and backward, but I cannot perceive him. . . . But . . . when he hath tried me, I shall come forth as gold." He is sure that his vindication will come. If not in this life, then in the life to come: "For I know that my redeemer liveth, and that he shall stand at the latter day upon the earth: and though after my skin worms destroy this body, yet in my flesh shall I see God."

GOD'S ANSWER AND JOB'S REPENTANCE

"The Lord answered Job out of the whirlwind." Job had not cursed God nor denied Him; but out of the depths of his suffering he had asked many difficult questions. Why, being innocent, had so great a calamity come upon him? And why, if he was called upon to suffer, was he not permitted to die? Why does God permit the righteous to suffer and the unrighteous to prosper?

Now God answers these questions. "The Lord answered Job out of the whirlwind." The striking fact, however, is that there is no reference in these answers to any of the questions asked by Job. The only answer is a series of questions addressed to Job, questions which humble him and remind him of the majesty and omnipotence of God: "Where wast thou when I laid the foundations of the earth, . . . when the morning stars sang together, and all the sons of God shouted for joy? . . . Who shut up the sea with doors? . . . Hast thou entered into the springs of the sea? . . . Hast thou entered into the treasures of the snow? . . . Have the gates of death been opened unto thee? . . . Canst thou bind the sweet influences of Pleiades or loose the bands of Orion? . . . Doth the hawk fly by thy wisdom, and stretch her wings toward the south? . . . Canst thou draw out leviathan with an hook?"

What was the meaning of these questions? The meaning was, and is, that if we know so little about the ways of God in nature, if His ways in nature are often to us inscrutable, it must not be thought a strange thing in our lives that there are mysteries of providence which we cannot understand. These questions spoken by God brought Job to repentance. He did not repent of any of those sins with which his friends had rashly charged him, for he had not been guilty of them; but he did repent of his questioning the ways of God in his life: "I have heard of thee by the hearing of the ear: but now mine eye seeth thee. Wherefore I abhor myself, and repent in dust and ashes."

Job is now restored to even greater prosperity than he enjoyed before. The supreme vindication of Job's faith and trust, and of his character, too, is set forth in the beautiful fact that the Lord tells his three friends to go to Job and offer a burnt offering and ask Job to pray for them, "for him will I accept: lest I deal with you after your folly."

Such, then, is the Story of Job. Such is the great answer to the ever-present problem of sorrow and suffering. The great book tells us that God is to be trusted and obeyed, rather than argued about or demonstrated. His ways may be to us past finding out, but we can say with Job, "Though he slay me, yet will I trust in him." As God's ways in nature are inscrutable, so there are mysteries of His providence in our lives. There were such in the life of Job, and when God answered Job out of the whirlwind, He did not explain to Job the meanings of those providences. Neither will He for us. Yet, like Job, we can say, "When he hath tried me, I shall come forth as gold."

Again, the great book tells us that life is a probation, a trial, but that the purpose of the trial is always good. After all, there is nothing unique or extraordinary about the sufferings of Job. These trials are repeated from age to age and from day to day. Within the past few days, in the usual round of pastoral experience I have come upon those who are suffering the same trials that Job suffered. One was a woman in a home for the aged who had lost her property through the treachery and dishonesty of those in whom she had put her trust. One was a mother who had bade good-by to her daughter as she drove off in the afternoon, and was awakened at midnight with tidings of an automobile wreck in which her daughter had been burned to death. Another mother had received a fateful telegram from the War Department. Then there was a teacher, recently retired after a long and honorable service in the public schools, suddenly gone blind. There you have three of the trials of Job—loss of property, loss of loved ones, loss of health. Time brings to all one or more of these trials.

The purpose of these trials, however, is always good. How true is that inspired comment of James: "Ye have heard of the patience of Job, and have seen the end of the Lord; that the Lord is very pitiful, and of tender mercy." Yes, that is it! The end of the Lord! In the midst of your trials, remember the end of the Lord. I have a friend in the ministry who, after he left the seminary, went out as a missionary to China. There he lost his eyesight. Since then wave after wave of adversity and affliction has broken over his life. His attractive wife died. His daughter was smitten with an incurable disease. The son in whom he had placed his hopes was suddenly taken from him. He himself has recently been afflicted again in his body. But sometime ago he said to a friend, "I would not ask to go back, or be as I was before, for I am happier now than I was then, because I know more now about God."

That was true of Job also, when he said, "I have heard of thee by the hearing of the ear: but now mine eye seeth thee." From all his trials Job emerged triumphant. All his hope and all his creed were summed up thus: "He knoweth the way that I take: when he hath tried me, I shall come forth as gold." Upon that sublime utterance of Job there flashes the magnificent light of the illumination of the Christian apostle, the Christian sufferer, who said, "And we know that all things work together for good to them that love God."

2

THE TRIAL OF ABRAHAM

Now I know that thou fearest God (Gen. 22:12).

The God of Abraham, and the God of Isaac, and the God of Jacob"—that is the noble refrain which rings in majesty through the Scriptures. Our God, the God of Jesus Christ, the God of redemption, the covenant-making and the covenant-keeping God, was, and is, the God of Abraham, for, as Jesus said to the Sadducees who questioned the future life, "He is not the God of the dead, but the God of the living."

In some respects the most impressive place in the Holy Land is Hebron and the cave of Machpelah where Abraham was buried. It is one of the authentic places of the Holy Land. We may not be certain about the Mount of Transfiguration or the exact site of the Nativity or the Crucifixion or the Resurrection, but when we look down through the iron grating in the floor of the mosque at Hebron and see the ever-burning light in the cave far beneath us, we can be sure that is the place where Abraham was buried, and after him Isaac and Jacob. The grave of every great character in human history is a place of profound and moving interest, because there was laid to rest the body which was the tabernacle of a mighty soul.

Abraham is great not only in himself but because he acts at the beginning of Hebrew history. Great men owe a part of their greatness to the times in which they live. In another century Cromwell might have been just another English squire,

18

Washington another Virginia planter, and Lincoln another country lawyer; but in the providence of God they were born in great periods of human history. So was it with Abraham. In him God divided mankind into two streams which flow through the ages and meet again at Calvary. The promise was that in him all nations of the earth should be blessed. That promise has been fulfilled. Today Arabs, Jews, Christians all revere the name of Abraham.

Abraham at Hebron and the Oaks of Mamre

The whole life of Abraham, from his call out of Ur of the Chaldees down to his death after his wanderings to and fro in the land of Canaan, was in a certain sense a trial of his faith. But there was a supreme test, and that was the offering up of Isaac. In many a man's life there will be one great affection, one great sorrow, and one great trial. Here, then, is the trial of Abraham.

It was eventide at Hebron. Abraham rested and meditated under the oaks in front of the black tents. At length the sound of the women's and children's voices was stilled. The silence was broken only by the tinkle of the bells of the sheep and cattle, or the sound of the gentle evening wind in the leaves of the oak trees. Now the stars came out. As he watched the stars, Abraham remembered the promise that had been given long ago that his seed would be as numerous as the stars. Since then many stars had risen and set. Many moons had waxed and waned. Many caravans had come up from Mesopotamia since then. Many a season the river Jordan had overflowed its banks. Many journeys had Abraham taken over the land, pitching his tents now here, now there, but never forgetting to build an altar to the Lord. Perhaps Abraham was beginning to wonder about the fulfillment of the promise that he was to possess the land. All the land had been promised to him, but all that he received, even down to the time of his death, was the cave of Machpelah, where, as he put it, "I may bury my dead out of my sight." Perhaps now there had come to Abraham some intimation that he was really seeking another and "a better country, that is, an heavenly," and "a city which hath foundations." But however it may have been with the land, the long-promised heir, Isaac, had at length been born. As he sat there that night beneath the oaks and beneath the stars, perhaps Abraham said to himself, "My race will soon be run, but in Isaac shall my seed be called. Yes, God is good. Through Isaac He will bless the generations to come. Blessed be God! 'His mercy is everlasting; and his truth endureth to all generations.'"

Then suddenly a voice spoke. Abraham knew that voice well. There was no doubt as to the Speaker. It was the voice of an old friend. But this time it spoke not of the destiny of the race which would spring from his loins, the star-like multitude of his descendants, or the blessings which his seed would bestow upon the whole family of nations. Now the voice spoke not of his hopes but of the frustration of his hopes, not of the increase of his race but of the annihilation of it, not of the blessing but of its withdrawal. "Take now thy son, thine only son Isaac, whom thou lovest, and get thee into the land of Moriah; and offer him there for a burnt offering upon one of the mountains which I tell thee of."

The inspired narrative relates only the command and Abraham's obedience to that command. What occurred between the hearing of that command and the start of the journey toward the land of Moriah is left to our imagination. What a night it was for Abraham! It must have seemed as if the earth were reeling beneath his feet, as if the symbolic stars were falling out of heaven. His only son! The son of the promise! And that son to be offered up for a burnt offering on the distant mountain! The shock to Abraham, however, was not so much moral—for such sacrifices were not uncommon then—as it was emotional, a deathblow to his hopes and expectations. Isaac was the son of his old age, and the affections of the aged father wound themselves all the more closely about the son of the promise. Then there was the shock to Abraham as a believer. It seemed now that the great hopes that he had entertained were to be frustrated. Why was the promise given only to be blighted? While Abraham struggled with that problem, one by one the stars and the constellations pitched their tents in the fields of space: the evening star, the Dog Star, Orion, the Pleiades, and at length the morning star. But when the day dawned Abraham had won his battle. The Jews have an interesting legend which, as in the case of Job, relates that Satan appeared in heaven to bring accusation against Abraham. His charge was that, now that God had blessed him with prosperity and with an heir, he had become selfish and prayerless and had forgotten God. As in the case of Job, God accepted the challenge of Satan and submitted Abraham to the trial of his faith.

Some of you will remember the delight and thrill you felt when one morning your father announced that he would take you with him on a long journey, perhaps to a distant city. So I imagine it was that day when Abraham told Isaac that he was going to take him with him to the land of Moriah. There was stir and bustle that morning in the kitchen, and outside there was the sound of the ax as the servants cut the faggots for the burnt offering. At length all things were ready. The faggots, the loaves, and the wine were upon the back of the ass and the other things upon the back of the servant. And so they started on their journey. Now and then they turned to look toward the black tents, growing indistinct in the distance, and they could still see Sarah standing at the opening of her tent, waving them a farewell. Isaac was all excitement and delight. But once when he looked up at his father he thought he saw the mark of pain on his face, and he asked him if he was ill.

On the third day Mount Moriah loomed up on the distant horizon. When they reached the foot of the mountain, the servant and the ass were left behind. The wood, the flint, the knife, and the thongs were placed on Isaac's back. Thus they ascended the mountain. Once, when they stopped to rest, Isaac said to his father, "Father, have you not forgotten something? Here is the wood and the fire, the knife, and the thongs with which to bind the sacrifice, and here are the ointment and the incense. But, Father, where is the lamb?" Was there ever such a question asked before? Or was there ever such an answer given? "God will provide," said Abraham, still hoping and still believing. Isaac no doubt wondered at the secrecy of his father, but he must have concluded that he had made some arrangements in advance for an animal for the sacrifice.

There they were now, on the top of the mountain, at the

place where David, much later, saw the angel stay the plague which had punished Israel for the sin of taking a census. Here one day was to arise the glorious temple of Solomon. Abraham and Isaac proceeded to build the altar. First, they leveled the ground off, then laid the stones one on top of the other, then the wood on the stones, and the flint by its side, and the knife also. Abraham was a great altar builder. Wherever he went, he built an altar to the Lord. Other men you can trace by their sins and their follies, Abraham by his altars. But never before had he built such an altar as this.

The altar was completed. Abraham stood gazing into the distance. To himself he said in his agony, "How can I give him up, the child of my old age, the symbol of the promise? How can I tell his mother that I laid my hand upon her child? How can I go down to old age without a son?" Then Isaac, having completed his work at the altar, interrupted Abraham, saying, "All things are ready now, Father. Here is the altar, here are the stones, the wood, and the fire; but still I see no animal for the sacrifice. Where shall we get the lamb?" Then Abraham, placing his hand on Isaac's shoulder, said to him with trembling voice, "Isaac, my son, you are the lamb! Three nights ago, Isaac, as I meditated beneath the oaks at Hebron, the Lord spoke to me, saying, 'Take now thy son, thine only son, Isaac, whom thou lovest, and get thee into the land of Moriah; and offer him there for a burnt offering upon one of the mountains which I will tell thee of.'"

In dealing with this sublime and moving scene, we must not forget the submission of Isaac. He might have seized the knife and struck his father down. But, as a true type of Christ, he opened not his mouth and lay down willingly upon the altar and was bound with the thongs. Abraham placed a farewell kiss on his brow, and then, holding the knife in his hand, he looked off into the distance. There was a moment of hesitation. Then the knife flashed in the sunlight as he lifted it on high; but before he could bring it down, he heard the voice of God, "Lay not thine hand upon the lad, . . . for now I know that thou fearest God." As he stood waiting, Abraham heard the struggle of a ram caught in the thicket by its horns. Immediately he cut the thongs which bound Isaac, and together they secured the ram and offered it as a sacrifice upon the altar. As Abraham came down from the mount, he named the place Jehovah-jireh, "the Lord will provide." Now the promise that had been given long before, but which had been contingent upon his complete submission and perfect obedience, was given again: "Because thou hast done this thing, and hast not withheld thy son, thine only son; that in blessing I will bless thee, and in multiplying I will multiply thy seed as the stars of the heaven. . . . And in thy seed shall all the nations of the earth be blessed: because thou hast obeyed my voice."

The chapter which relates this extraordinary scene on Mount Moriah begins with these words: "And it came to pass after these things, that God did tempt Abraham." All of us, too, He tempts, in the same sense of the word, not to do evil, but in the sense that He tries us to see what is in our hearts. Abraham was tested with his dearest possession, his son of the promise. He stood the test well, as Job did his, and God said to him, "Now I know that thou fearest God, seeing thou hast not withheld thy son, thine only son, from me." I used to wonder, driving into cemeteries on my pastoral duties, why there are so many which bear the name Mount Moriah. But the reason is not difficult to see. There in Christian faith and trust many a believing father and mother had, as it were, offered up their children. During a war many a parent is put to the test of Abraham. Thousands upon thousands of American fathers and mothers have climbed the steep and lonely path to Moriah, where they met the supreme test. What did God find in their hearts?

On the way up to the top of the mountain, when Isaac asked Abraham, "Where is the lamb?" Abraham answered in sublime faith, "God will provide." God never forgets or forsakes the believing and trusting soul. Abraham expressed his faith to the uttermost in God, and God did not fail him. "By faith Abraham, when he was tried, offered up Isaac: . . . accounting that God was able to raise him up, even from the dead." God did not fail him. As Abraham's day was, so was his strength.

From Moriah one can see Calvary. Centuries later, behold another procession winding its way up the hill to Calvary. Three condemned criminals, each bearing his cross, march along the road. Urged forward by the lashes of the soldiers, cursed and jeered by the mob, Jesus, naked and bleeding and crowned with thorns, marches to Calvary. Like Isaac, He is obedient to His Father. In Gethsemane He prays, "If it be possible, let this cup pass from me! Nevertheless, not as I will, but as thou wilt."

On the cross He cries out, "My God, my God, why hast thou forsaken me?" The mob shouts for another miracle. "Ah, thou that opened the eyes of the blind and cleansed the leper and raised the dead, come, give us another miracle! Come down from the cross, and we will believe on thee!" But from the cross He would not come down. Not the nails that they had driven through His hands and feet, but love held Him fast to the cross.

Thus Moriah looked forward to the great scene on Calvary where Christ laid down His life. "While we were yet sinners, Christ died for us." May that wondrous love warm and guard all our hearts, and tell us that a wise, tender, forgiving, and loving God is ever near to us. Because we know that to be true, we can say with another man who stood well his trial: "Who shall separate us from the love of Christ? shall tribulation, or distress, or persecution, or famine, or nakedness, or peril, or sword? . . . No, in all these things we are more than conquerors, through him that loved us." Abraham, David, Paul, all the saints and martyrs, all you who came off conquerors and more than conquerors through Him that loved us, speak now to our souls! Awaken faith within us! Invite us to climb these Delectable Mountains upon which your feet are now standing, and let us join the company of those who through faith came off conquerors and more than conquerors through Him who on the cursed tree loved us with that unutterable and everlasting love!

3

THE TRIAL OF JACOB

And there wrestled a man with him until the
breaking of the day (Gen. 32:24).

Undoubtedly some great thing happened here to Jacob. He passed through some great change, experienced some great blessing. But just what it was we cannot know. Jacob himself was unable to tell all that had happened to him, for when he asked his mysterious antagonist, "Tell me, I pray thee, thy name," the wrestler answered, "Wherefore is it that thou dost ask after my name?" Yet when the struggle was over and the angel had departed, life was never again the same for Jacob. He tells us what he had passed through, what he had experienced, by the name that he gave to the place where he had wrestled with the angel. "Peniel," he called it—"I have seen God face to face."

A man and an angel wrestling! I wonder if that is a history of every man's life. God wrestling with man, trying to bring out the spiritual and the heavenly and the eternal that is in him, and man wrestling with God, resisting God and His Holy Spirit, until in humility and weakness he cries out, "I will not let thee go, except thou bless me!" Michael and the Devil disputed with one another for the body of Moses. So good and evil, heaven and earth, wrestle with one another for the possession of a man's soul.

Sin casts a long shadow, longer than the sinner ever imagines

at the time he sins. It was twenty years, almost a whole generation as men count time, since Jacob had fled the land of Canaan
after deceiving his father and defrauding his brother Esau. At
Bethel, on the way down to Mesopotamia, he had had the
wonderful vision of a ladder let down from heaven and the
angels of God ascending and descending. But since then Jacob
had not seen much of the angels. He had, however, found a
human angel. The lovely daughter of Laban, drawing water
for her flocks at the well, immediately won all the affection
and devotion in Jacob's heart. For fourteen years he had toiled
for her hand, and all these years her smile had been the star of
his hope.

Now, after twenty years, Jacob was on his way back to his
father's country—a Jacob quite different from the solitary fu-
gitive who had fled from his father's encampment with nothing but his staff in his hand. Now he was a prosperous man.
He had wrestled with Laban, and had won. He had wrestled
with the world and fortune, and had come off victorious. With
numerous flocks and herds and his wives and children and
followers, Jacob was on his way back to Canaan. And yet he
was uneasy and unhappy. Why? Because he was approaching
the borderland of Seir, where his brother Esau lived. When he
thought of Esau, Jacob remembered the mean crime he had
committed against him and was uneasy and afraid. He had
thought little about it during the twenty years in which he
wrestled with the world and prosperity in the home of Laban.
Daily events and cares, and pleasures, and dangers had seemed
to blot out the memory of transgression and sin. But now,
suddenly, that memory awakened!

Twenty years! "Surely," Jacob thought to himself, "that is
long enough to dull Esau's memory of what I did to him. He
has now become a great man himself, and will have forgotten
the mean trick that I did to him." And yet Jacob knew that he
himself had not forgotten. No; the one sinned against might
forget, but not the one who sinned. Sin and remorse are not
subject to time. They are timeless, ageless. The sin that a man
commits today, when conscience and memory bring it back to
him twenty years from today, yes, fifty or seventy years
from today, will be as fresh as it was twenty seconds after he

committed the sin. "Be sure your sin will find you out!" The likelihood is that it will find a man out in time, as Jacob feared that his sin was finding him out. It will find him out in conscience, as Jacob's sin found him out as he drew near to the borders of Seir. It will find a man out, finally, inevitably, inexorably, in eternity.

Jacob had sent messengers ahead to sound out Esau and to ask grace in his sight. The messengers returned with the grim tidings, "We came to thy brother Esau, and also he cometh to meet thee, and four hundred men with him." When Jacob heard that, he was all the more afraid, and he called upon God in prayer: "O God of my father Abraham, and God of my father Isaac, . . . deliver me, I pray thee, from the hand of my brother, from the hand of Esau: for I fear him, lest he will come and smite me, and the mother with the children."

Frightened though he was, Jacob's relative shrewdness did not forsake him in this crisis. He divided his people and his flocks and herds into two bands and sent them on across the brook Jabbok ahead of him, his thought being that if Esau fell upon one of these bands, the other might possibly escape. Thus his flocks and herds and wives and children and all his possessions crossed the Jabbok and disappeared in the distance, until even the faintest tinkle of a bell on one of the goats was no longer heard. But Jacob himself waited on the other side of the Jabbok. Some mysterious influence held him back and detained him there. "Jacob was left alone." The highest spiritual blessings and the greatest changes may come when a man is left alone. In this instance God must speak with Jacob alone. He says to him, "Be still, and know that I am God." In this hour, in this night, Jacob is left alone. He is not to hear the lowing of his herds, the cries of the little children, nor the affectionate voice of the beloved Rachel. From all that he is separated, shut out.

Wondering what is in store for him, filled with dread at the approach of Esau, and also with a nameless dread of something else, something different and greater, Jacob waits there on the banks of the Jabbok. Night falls. The stars one by one come out and the evening wind begins to stir in the tops of the trees. Suddenly, Jacob finds himself in the grip of a strong adversary.

With all his impulse and energy he turns to grapple with him. He cannot discern his features in the shadows of the night, and wonders who it is that has seized him. Perhaps he thinks that Esau has stolen a march on him and now has come to execute vengeance on him. But whoever it is—Esau or some other—Jacob enters into the battle with all his energy and strength. Nothing is heard save the scraping of their feet upon the stones and the explosion of their breath, as the two antagonists struggle to and fro in one another's grip.

All night they wrestle to and fro. Neither can get the upper hand. But at length the mysterious antagonist puts forth his hand and touches the thigh of Jacob. The pivot control of Jacob's body is lost, and in a moment he is weak, halt, and lame. Yet he does not give up the struggle. With desperation he holds on to his stronger adversary. It is beginning to dawn upon him now that this is no ordinary antagonist. Here is one who may have the power to bless him!

When the light of the morning begins to appear over the desert and through the trees on the bank of the brook, the angel, hasting to get home, says to Jacob, "Let me go, for the day breaketh!" But Jacob answers, "I will not let thee go, except thou bless me!" The angel surrenders to Jacob's instant prayer and blesses him with a change of name and a change of heart. He says to Jacob, "What is thy name?" and he answers "Jacob." Then the angel says, "Thy name shall be called no more Jacob"—the supplanter, the grasper of your brother's heel—"but Israel" —a prince with God.

Jacob always made a happy choice in the names he gave to places. The place where he had seen the angels ascending the golden ladder he called Bethel, "the house of God." This place where he had wrestled all night with the angel, and where he had been blessed with a change of name and heart he called Peniel, "I have seen God face to face."

This mysterious encounter, when, as Hosea puts it, Jacob wept and "had power over the angel," shows some of the ways in which spiritual changes are wrought in man. One of these ways is by adversity and trial. Here adversity and trial issue in a change of heart and in newness of strength. That was a painful, desperate, terrifying, all-night struggle that Jacob had with his adversary, but before it was over, he discovered that the midnight wrestler had power to bless him. Jacob still struggled with him; but he struggled now, not to overcome him, but to hold him, to retain him, to secure a blessing from him. "I will not let thee go, except thou bless me."

The one whom Jacob took to be an enemy seeking to destroy him turned out to be a friend with power to help him. So it often is in life. That night when the disciples had been sent across the sea by themselves while Jesus remained on the mountain, and the terrible storm broke over them and they thought they were going to perish—that night at the fourth watch, the hour before the dawn, when human energies are at their lowest and it is easy to yield to fear and despair, they saw one walking like a specter across the sea toward them. When they saw this ghost, the disciples cried out in terror, thinking it was coming to sink them and send them to the bottom. They had thought they were going to perish in the storm, but something far worse was coming upon them. A ghost! They were fishermen and sailors, and they could battle with a storm. But what could they do with a ghost? Ready to jump into the sea rather than face that ghost, they suddenly heard a voice, "Be of good cheer; it is I." How their hearts must have rejoiced when they heard that voice which they had heard so many times before, which they knew so well and could never forget, saying to them, "Be of good cheer; it is I; be not afraid!" Now, instead of trying to row away in terror from the approaching demon, the disciples rested on their oars and received Christ into the ship, and "immediately the ship was at the land whither they went."

Often God's providences will appear to us something other than what they really are. To the anxious and troubled heart they may seem hostile and dangerous, as Jesus on that stormy night seemed to His disciples to be a specter, a ghost. But soon they discovered that the ghost was their friend and Master, and all their fears were gone when they heard Him say, "Be of good cheer; it is I; be not afraid." Jacob thought that the midnight wrestler was some dangerous enemy who had laid hold on him to take his life. Instead of that, he discovered that he was a friend who had come to give him more abundant life. So behind a frowning providence God often hides a shining face.

Joseph, in Egypt, sold by his brethren, a slave in Potiphar's household, falsely accused of sin and crime and cast into the prison, might well have thought that all these things were against him. But in the end he discovered that they were with him and for him, and that the iron had entered into his soul only to make his name blessed to Israel and to the generations to come.

Sometimes men wrestle with sorrow as with a dangerous adversary, only to find out in the end that the sorrow through which they have passed was their friend. One of the most notable preachers of the last century, William M. Taylor, relates how he left his home in Liverpool to fill an engagement in Glasgow. As he left the house to go to the station, the last sight on which his eye rested was that of his little daughter held up at the window in her grandmother's arms. As the carriage drove off, the child waved her father a fond and laughing farewell. Many a time, he said, during the railroad trip to Glasgow that vision of his little daughter rose up before his memory and filled his heart with joy. But he was never to see her again. The next morning he was stunned by a telegram which told of her sudden death. At first it seemed to him a blow that staggered his faith and crushed his hopes and put out the lamp of his joy. But as the years went by and the vision of that child waving him farewell came back to him, it seemed to him as if God had set her in the window of heaven to beckon him upward to his eternal home. "I would not give that memory for all the gold on earth," he said. "I would not part with the inspiration which it stirs within me for all that the world could bestow."

The result of Jacob's experience that night was a new knowledge of God, and that is life's great blessing: that we should know God and put our trust in Him. Jacob named the place where he had this experience Peniel, "I have seen God face to face." He had thought he had seen God and heard Him twenty years before when he had had that dream at Bethel, and he *had* seen Him and heard Him. But now he had seen God in a new way. That, too, was the experience of Job. "Oh that I knew where I might find him!" cried Job, "that I might come even to his seat!" But at the end of his trial this is what he said: "I have heard of thee by the hearing of the ear: but now mine eye seeth thee."

This night when he wrestled with the angel marked the turning point, a change, in the life of Jacob. There were other events, no doubt, that prepared for it, but this was the decisive night. There is such a turning point in the history of the soul. On some journey you have felt as you went along that you had turned into the wrong road. Yet you were not quite sure, and you continued driving or walking along the road. At length you came to a dead end, or some other intimation that you were certainly off the road, and you turned about and went back. That was the turning point. Although the incidents that had gone before had prepared you for it, there was a definite moment when you turned about. So is it with repentance, with conversion, and with the new birth. The change came for Jacob when, weak and halt and lame, he made that prayer: "I will not let thee go, except thou bless me."

Jacob was determined that the angel should not escape him until he had blessed him. Even in his dealings with Esau, shady and disreputable though they were, he had been eager for a spiritual blessing. Here, as Hosea puts it, "he had power over the angel, and prevailed; he wept." How hard do you struggle with your angel? The same angel comes to struggle with you and has the same power to bless you; but your pride, your self-sufficiency, your self-righteousness, must first be overcome. Do you resist the Holy Spirit? Do you strive against the angel? Or will you strive now to hold him? And will you say to God who speaks to you by His Holy Spirit in the midnight struggles, in the sorrows of life, in the midday light and happiness and joy, "I will not let thee go, except thou bless me"?

> The moon looked down on Jabbok's rill,
>   Where Jacob waited full of dread;
> The wind awoke, and then was still;
>   Orion soon would leave his bed.
>
> Then suddenly an angel came
>   And wrestled with the waiting man;
> Who sought in vain to learn his name,
>   Or his mysterious features scan.

All night they wrestled to and fro;
　Nor man nor angel could prevail;
Neither would let the other go,
　Till Jacob's strength began to fail.

The angel touched him on the thigh,
　While Jacob struggled, halt and lame,
And, panting, lifted up his cry,
　"Tell me thy nature and thy name!"

Then as the night began to wear,
　The angel, hasting to be home,
Surrendered to his instant prayer,
　And blessed him with a change of name.

"Thou art," he said, "a rogue no more;
　Proud battler with thy staff and rod,
Supplanter of another's store;
　But Israel, a prince with God!"

O Midnight Wrestler by the brook,
　Whose potent touch brings souls alive,
Come, cast on me thy mighty look,
　And in my heart thy light revive.[1]

---

1. Clarence Edward Macartney

4

THE TRIAL OF JOSEPH

The iron entered into his soul
(Psalm 105:18, The Book of Common Prayer).

A very interesting fact, that: the man whose life makes one of the world's greatest stories was a man into whose soul the iron had entered. No one would take an interest in a life that was all sunshine, happiness, and success. The greatness of life does not-come out until the soul feels the touch of iron. Ambition, youth, beauty, temptation, suffering, sorrow, jealousy, hate, forgiveness—all the great elements for the great story are here in the life of Joseph. The reason for the world-wide popularity of Joseph and his story is to be found in his youth, his dreams, his ambition, his trials, his magnanimity, and his sense of the divinity that shaped his rough-hewn ends.

When the prodigal son was returning from the "far country," while he was yet a great way off, his father saw him. Love magnifies and increases the vision of a man's eye. But so also does hate. That morning when Joseph came to visit his brothers to see how they did, his coat of many colors brushing the tears from the cheeks of the morning flowers, his brothers saw him afar off. One of them, standing near the campfire, saw something moving far to the north and east, this side of the mountains. He watched it for a little, and then, catching a flash of one of the colors of the coat, turned to his brothers and said, "Behold, this dreamer cometh. Come . . . let us slay him, and cast him into some pit; . . . and we shall see what will become of his dreams!"

The whole history of Joseph, from that morning when his brothers saw him coming to visit them down to the end, is a wonderful mosaic of divine providence. Let us see how that was. When he left his father's home at Hebron, Jacob told Joseph to visit his brothers in Shechem; but when he got to Shechem he could not find them. A man who found him wandering in the fields told him that they had left some time before and that he heard them saying they were going to Dothan. If they had remained in Shechem, or had gone to some other section, all would have been different. But they went to Dothan, which lay on the caravan route to Egypt. Reuben, the oldest of the brothers, and apparently the most tenderhearted, tried to save the life of Joseph. "Shed no blood, but cast him into this pit," he urged, giving his brothers the impression that they could get rid of him that way without actually shedding blood. But his plan was, when the chance came, to save the life of Joseph.

When they had cast him into the pit, the hardhearted brothers sat down to eat as if nothing had happened, and Reuben went off to attend to some business with his flock. But while he was absent, the caravan of the Ishmaelites hove in sight, and at the suggestion of Judah Joseph was sold to the Ishmaelites. The caravan was hardly out of sight before Reuben returned, only to find that Joseph was gone. If Reuben had come back a half-hour sooner than he did, or if the caravan had come a half-hour later, or if it had been bound northward instead of southward toward Egypt, then Joseph would not have been carried down into Egypt, and the whole history would have been different. If in Egypt he had been sold as a slave to some one other than Potiphar, an officer of Pharaoh's household, or had been tempted by some woman other than Potiphar's wife, his whole history would have been different. Again, if he had been cast into prison a month earlier or a month later, he would not have met that chief butler, whose dream he interpreted and who finally spoke for him to Pharaoh, and might have stayed in the prison for the rest of his life. When Joseph looked back upon that whole wonderful history, he said to his brothers, "It was not you that sent me hither, but God."

THE TRIAL BY TEMPTATION

All the world loves a dreamer, and yet at the same time the world conspires against the dreamer. It will do what it can to persuade the dreamer to forsake his dreams or, what is still sadder, to make him unworthy of them. Come, now, let us see what will become of Joseph's dream.

In the house of Potiphar, Joseph was the occasion of blessing and prosperity to that house. "The Lord blessed the Egyptian's house for Joseph's sake." "For David's sake" is one of the beautiful phrases that God frequently speaks in the Bible. For some "Joseph's sake" many a house and many a soul has been blessed.

The great story would not have been complete without trial by temptation. In the Greek tale Hercules was confronted at the turning of the road by two women. One, a beautiful but wanton woman, invited him to go with her and promised him pleasure, ease, and delight. The other, a woman of modest and severe countenance, also invited Hercules to go with her, telling him that her path and company would be hard and difficult, but that they would lead to strength and honor. The prelude to the great ministry of Jesus was when the Holy Spirit drove Him into the wilderness to be tempted of the Devil. There is no wall high enough to keep out temptation from a man's life. Temptation, especially at Joseph's time of life, has a determining influence. What a man does then, what he accepts or rejects, what he chooses or dismisses, will influence his life ever after. In the hot fires of temptation many a man's dreams have vanished.

This was no ordinary temptation. Joseph was not a stone, a mummy, but a red-blooded young man in his late twenties. It was not one temptation on one day, but a repeated temptation. Then there was the high rank of the temptress and the natural inclination to feel flattered by her invitation. There was the chance, too, for an easy life and promotion. Again, there was danger in refusal, for

Heaven has no rage like love to hatred turned,
Nor hell a fury like a woman scorned.

Everything was on the side of Joseph's yielding to that temptation. Yet, in spite of the odds against him, it was Joseph who conquered, not the temptation. The secret of his victory was the fear of God. All other considerations would have failed, all other anchors would have dragged, but not the fear of God. Joseph was loyal to the master who had bought him, and who had honored him by promotion and by his confidence. But it was not that sense of loyalty to Potiphar, nor the dread of Potiphar's anger if he should yield and be discovered, that saved Joseph. It was his loyalty to conscience and God. An old story tells how when Joseph began to talk about God to the temptress, she flung her skirt over the bust of the god that stood in the chamber and said, "Now, God will not see!" But Joseph answered, "My God sees!" He lived under the power and authority of that great sentence that he uttered, "How then can I do this great wickedness, and sin against God?" Today, thirty-six centuries after Joseph said that, in a pulpit in a part of the world not then known to be in existence a minister repeats that magnificent utterance for the benefit of others.

THE TRIAL OF ADVERSITY

Joseph has survived the first fiery trial, the temptation of the flesh. His faith was able to remove that mountain. Now he is qualified for greater things; but there is still another trial.

Joseph's loyalty to God and conscience resulted in his being cast into prison. That, apparently, was his only reward. Can you imagine how Joseph felt that first night in the prison? Did he hear a voice saying, "Joseph, you have acted like a fool. If you had yielded to that temptation, you would now be living in ease and honor instead of lying here in this stinking prison"? What did Joseph think or say? Was he tempted to ask, "Does it pay to be good"? Was he tempted to exclaim, "O Virtue, thou art but an empty name"? What we know is that the Lord was with Joseph in the prison and showed him mercy. That is

a great line coming near the end of the passage which relates
Joseph's temptation, his resistance, and his being cast into
prison: "And he was there in the prison. But the Lord was with
Joseph." And still he is with all those who stand with God and
conscience.

Joseph had not been soured by his misfortune, or cast into
despair by his adversity, but resolved to make the best of his
lot and do what he could to help other prisoners. The outcome was that in a short time Joseph was made chief deputy
by the keeper of the prison. Then came the dreams of the
chief baker and the chief butler. Joseph was able to interpret
those dreams because he had been true to his own. The chief
butler had dreamed that Pharaoh's cup was in his hand and
that he took grapes from three vine branches and pressed
them into Pharaoh's cup and gave the cup into Pharaoh's
hand. Joseph told him the interpretation of it was that the
three branches he had seen were three days, and that within
three days Pharaoh would lift up his head and restore him to
his place, and he would again deliver Pharaoh's cup into his
hand.

In three days the dream came true. The chief baker was
hanged, but the chief butler was pardoned and restored to his
post. As the butler was leaving the dungeon that day Joseph—and this was as near as he ever came to breaking down—
said to him, "Think on me when it shall be well with thee,
and shew kindness, I pray thee, unto me; and make mention
of me unto Pharaoh, and bring me out of this house: for
indeed I was stolen away out of the land of the Hebrews; and
here also have I done nothing that they should put me into
the dungeon." Then the key was turned in the lock of the
prison door. It opened for a little to let the chief butler out
and then closed again. What did Joseph think then? Did
another voice say to him: "Joseph, you have played the fool.
Did not that brief glance you had of the blue Egyptian sky
look good to you when they opened the door to let the chief
butler out? You have played the fool. If you had only yielded
to that temptation, you would now be out in the bright Egyptian sunlight like that chief butler. You will never hear from
him again, in spite of his promises."

THE TRIAL OF PROSPERITY

It did, indeed, look as if Joseph would never hear from the chief butler. "Yet did not the chief butler remember Joseph, but forgat him." When finally he did remember Joseph, it was apparently not out of gratitude to him, but that he might rise with Pharaoh. Pharaoh had dreamed in the night, and no one could interpret his dreams. He had seen seven well-favored cattle come out of the Nile and feed in a meadow. After them, seven lean cattle came out of the river and ate up the seven well-favored kine. In the second dream Pharaoh saw seven ears of corn, good ears, come out from one stock. After them came up seven thin ears, blasted with the east wind, and the seven thin ears devoured the seven good ears. The chief butler told Pharaoh about his experience with Joseph in the prison and how he had interpreted his dreams for him. This led to Joseph's being summoned out of the dungeon into Pharaoh's presence.

When he heard Pharaoh relate his dreams, which none of the magicians could interpret, Joseph told him that the dreams predicted the seven years of plenty to be followed by seven years of famine. He counseled Pharaoh to choose out a discreet and wise administrator and set him over the land of Egypt. He was to gather during the good years all the grain that could be secured and lay it up in storehouses against the days of want and famine. The one whom Pharaoh selected to be his food administrator was none other than Joseph. Pharaoh put his ring on Joseph's hand, fine vestures on his body, a gold collar about his neck, and gave him a chariot in which to ride. Whenever Joseph went out on business of state, slaves and outriders ran ahead of him shouting to the people, "Bow the knee! Joseph is coming!" All this favor was crowned by his marriage to the beautiful daughter of the priest of On. Only thirty years of age, and Joseph has gone as high as a man could go in all Egypt, after Pharaoh himself.

Joseph was soon to be tested by a more searching test than the iron of adversity. He was to be tested by prosperity. What effect does prosperity have on the souls of many men? One effect is pride. That was the effect it had on Nebuchadnezzar, who walked on the roof garden of his palace at sunset, saw the tawny Euphrates flowing through the city, the one hundred and fifty brass gates, the colossal walls, the beautiful hanging gardens he had built for his bride, and said to himself, "Is not this great Babylon, that I have built?" Another effect of prosperity is that it often makes men hard and selfish. The more they have been blessed in life, the less they want to share their blessings with others. Again, it often makes men forget the friends of their humble youth, and worst of all, it makes men forget God.

But Joseph stood this acid test of prosperity. He was not hard and selfish or proud, but the same simple, warmhearted, affectionate Joseph that he had always been. Neither did his prosperity make him forget his family and his father's house. When, indeed, he called one of his sons Manasseh, "for God . . . hath made me forget all my toil, and all my father's house," what he meant was that by the grace of God he had been able to forget the trials and troubles through which he had passed. But his later actions proved that he had never really forgotten his father or his eleven brothers. Pharaoh changed the name of Joseph to an Egyptian name, but he could not change his heart. The heart of Joseph always dwelt in the highlands of Canaan.

There were days when officers would come to Joseph, the prime minister, and ask him a question, and they would wonder why he did not answer. It was because Joseph was asking himself questions: "My father? Benjamin? My younger brother? And the ten brothers who sold me into Egypt? Do they still live? Do they ever think of Joseph? Does their conscience ever smite them?" There were days, too, when Joseph's beautiful wife, the daughter of the priest of On, putting her arm about Joseph would say, "Joseph, what are you thinking about? And why that faraway look in your eyes? Is my love and the love of your two sons not enough for you?" Yes; Joseph's thoughts oftentimes ranged far from Egypt. The bowing servants, the rigid lines of waiting soldiers, the gilded chariots, the red sandstone palaces, the fountains climbing the ladder of the sun—all that passed from his view, and what he saw was the black tents under the oaks at Hebron and the faces of Jacob and Benjamin and his ten brothers. Joseph was an exile from home, but splendor dazzled him in vain.

No; Joseph had never forgotten his father's house. Adversity had not alienated his heart from his father and brothers. They were shepherds, and shepherds were held in abomination by all Egyptians, but prosperity and rank never made Joseph ashamed of them. At length came that great scene of reconciliation, when Joseph, after those repeated scenes of pretended gruffness and severity, at length disclosed himself to his brothers and wept over them, and they over him, until all the Egyptians heard them, a scene not to be matched until sinners are reconciled to God in heaven amid the songs of rejoicing angels.

Tried by adversity, Joseph was not embittered. Tried by hate and cruelty, he answered with love and good will. His power and rank never tempted him to take vengeance upon the brothers who had so cruelly treated him. One of the hardest trials of life, and one of the severest tests, is to be ill-used, unnaturally used, by your own flesh and blood. Alas, how many embittered hearts I have come upon in this world who had failed to pass that test, who had answered hate with hate, and bitterness with bitterness! But Joseph forgave his brethren. Before Christ taught it, before Paul taught it, this great Christian of the Old Testament returned good for evil, loved his enemies, did good to them that despitefully used him, and so heaped coals of fire upon their heads. Are you troubled or embittered by the ill-treatment of your friends, your own flesh and blood? Then I yield the pulpit now to Joseph. Come, Joseph; come up the pulpit stairs, in that coat of many colors, and preach to us on the beauty of forgiveness!

The secret of Joseph's unfailing optimism, his kindness, and his readiness to forgive his enemies, was his faith in God. His brothers were frightened when he first disclosed himself to them. Their conscience smote them, and they dreaded his vengeance. But Joseph said to them, "Be not grieved, nor angry with yourselves, that ye sold me hither; for God did send me before you, to preserve life." Then again, after the death of Jacob, the brothers came to Joseph and, fearing that he would now take vengeance on them, gave him what they said was the dying request of Jacob—but which was probably forged—that Joseph should forgive his brethren. Joseph wept and said, "Am I in the place of God? But as for you, ye thought evil against me; but God meant it unto good." That was what life had taught Joseph: that whatever things had happened to him, even out of the bitterness of the enmity of others, God always meant it for his good. It was Paul who said, in one of his great passages, "All things work together for good to them that love God." But the world did not need to wait for Paul to sound that majestic note. Ages before, Joseph, triumphant in his great trial, said the same thing when he said, "As for you, ye thought evil against me; but God meant it unto good." Victor in life, indeed, is he who has learned that lesson! Is that what your life is teaching you? What effect has God's providence had upon your life? Is it making you humble, courageous, trusting, forgiving, loving, a believer in that Son of God, our Savior Jesus Christ, who came to die for you on the cross, and who in his wise providence has brought you to hear the story of God's redeeming love?

"Behold, this dreamer cometh!" Come again, Joseph, into our midst, for never can you come too often. Put on again that coat of many colors, woven in the web of providence, that coat which has in its strands all the colors of trial, adversity, temptation, forgiveness, purity, faith, triumph. Come, tell us of your victory over temptation, and how by the fear of God you kept your soul unstained and unpolluted. Come, let us hear you weep again over those cruel brothers who had wronged you, and so teach us how to love and how to forgive. Come, tell us of your faith. Teach us that God is in our life, that our times are in His hands, and that to them that love God and trust Him all things work together for good. Come, great Christian of the Old Testament, and by your life—its trials, its pits, its prisons, it sorrows, its temptations, its overcomings—tell us of that Savior who loved His brethren when they were sinners, and who went down into the Egypt of captivity and death that He might redeem them and present them faultless to God His father.

5

THE TRIAL OF MOSES

Thou shalt not go over thither (Deut. 34:4).

God's last word to Moses, after his heroic life and magnificent service, was No. Moses asked to go over the Jordan with the children of Israel into the land of Canaan, but God said, "Thou shalt not go over!"

In front of the church of the Huguenots in Paris, the Oratoire, is the noble statue of the great Protestant hero, Admiral de Coligny. At the base of the statue are the words spoken of Moses by the writer of the Letter to the Hebrews: "He endured, as seeing him who is invisible." Some men are governed by the temporal and by the seen, the visible. Moses was one of those great souls who are ruled and governed by the Invisible.

The three greatest men of the Bible are Abraham, Paul, and Moses. When I say this, I do not mean that in every instance these three men, in and of themselves, are the greatest men of the Bible. Their importance is in the streams of influences which flowed from them and the place they occupied in critical and formative periods of man's history. Even outside of the Bible the imprint of Moses is deep and lasting. Jude, writing as if it were a well-accepted fact in his day, speaks of how Michael and the Devil disputed over the body of Moses. For heaven and for the Devil, Moses was a great prize. Perhaps God gave him secret burial on Nebo's lonely mountain lest men should worship his sepulcher. Again, there is the beautiful Jewish legend of how the angel of death tried in vain to take the soul of Moses from him. Then God came down and drew the soul of Moses from him with a kiss. If anyone in the Bible deserved the kiss of God's approval, that man was Moses.

The whole life of Moses was a trial. And so life for all of us is a trial. But there was one supreme and final trial for Moses. To understand the power of that trial, we must review some of the incidents in his life. In this respect we are fortunate, because, in contrast with Elijah, Jeremiah, Isaiah, Paul, and other great men of the Bible, we are permitted to follow the earthly life of Moses from his cradle in the bending reeds of the Nile to his grave on Nebo's lonely mountain.

DIVINE PROVIDENCE

The first fact in the life of Moses is the providence of God. God has a plan and a work for every man. In a striking way we see God's plan in the life of Moses. A Pharaoh who "knew not Joseph" had arisen in Egypt, four hundred years after Jacob had gone down into Egypt at the invitation of Joseph. During these four centuries the little band of immigrants had multiplied greatly. Pharaoh tried to stop the plan of God for Israel. His first decree was that every male child should be put to death at birth. Thus he hoped to reduce the population of Israel. But there was one thing upon which Pharaoh had not counted. Oppressors of mankind and antagonists of God always leave out something in their evil conspiracies. What Pharaoh had not counted on was the fear of God in the heart of the midwives. "But the midwives feared God, and did not as the king of Egypt commanded them, but saved the men children alive." Then came the decree that every son that was born should be cast into the Nile. But in the providence of God it was that very Nile River, designed to be the death of Israel, which was to be the appointed means of saving Moses alive, and through him, the whole nation of Israel.

The birth of a child is always a stirring and solemnizing event. How much more so the birth of a child at this time, when all male infants were doomed to death! As the parents rejoiced that to them a child was given and a son was born, their joy was tempered by the reflection that by the decree of Pharaoh that child was doomed to death. Thus joy and sorrow, hope and dread, spread their wings over the cradle of Moses. His parents saw that he was a goodly child, and that all the more determined them to do what they could to deliver him from the hand of Pharaoh. Fortunately, most parents see their newborn child as a goodly child and do what they can to hide him and protect him from the sorrow, pain, and woe and violence of this world. For three months the birth of Moses was kept secret. You can imagine how they managed that. You can see them hastily carrying the child into the inmost chamber of the house and closing all the doors whenever an Egyptian officer or inspector passed down the street.

But after three months, with the child growing from day to day and his voice becoming stronger, it was no longer possible to conceal him in the home. Then it was they made an ark of bulrushes and daubed it with slime and pitch and, putting the child in this cradle, carried him in the night to the banks of the river and set the cradle afloat on the breast of the Nile. You can see the farewell of the parents: the repeated kisses that the mother bestowed upon the little child in that cradle, again and again going up the bank of the river and then back to the cradle to kiss the child once more, until the father, Amram, warned her that the sun was rising and they must be off. But they left his sister Miriam as a sentinel hidden in the bushes near the river.

A babe floating in a cradle on the bosom of the mighty river, with the reeds bending over him, perhaps a lazy crocodile eyeing him! Here we have the incarnation of what seems to be helplessness, defenselessness; and yet that infant is safe. No weapon formed against him shall prosper, for upon his brow is the mark of God's eternal purpose and invincible plan. The very river which Pharaoh decreed to compass his destruction, now, under the providence of God, becomes the means of his salvation and deliverance.

That morning, the daughter of Pharaoh came down to the river to bathe with her servants and maids. From the few touches given us in the sketch of this princess, we take it that she was childless and that, like most women, she had a yearning for a child. When she came to bathe in the river, she happened to come down to the very place where Moses lay crooning in his ark of bulrushes. If she had chosen to bathe that day on the other side of the Nile, or one hundred yards up or down the river, or around that bend behind those palm trees, then Moses would not have been seen, and the history of Israel and the history of the world would have been different. But there are no "ifs," there are no slips in God's wonderful plan. There was only one place on all the Nile River where the daughter of Pharaoh could have gone down to bathe on that particular day, and that was that very place where Moses lay in his little ark with the reeds of the river bending over him.

THE FIRST TRIAL OF MOSES

So far, Moses had played a great, but involuntary, part in the plan of God for him, for Israel, and for mankind. But now we come to the event in his life where he, himself, by his own decision, chose the plan of God for himself. The first trial of Moses came when he was asked to choose between the splendor and riches of Egypt and affliction with the people of God. Here we discern a principle of every true and good life. There comes a decision, a choice, an eleventh hour verdict, a parting of the road, and henceforth the energies of the soul are directed toward the right side. Moses made that choice. In human destiny there are two elements: God's purpose and plan and man's free choice, when he chooses for himself and wills for himself that which God has willed for him.

I wish I had been there that day in the palace of Pharaoh when Moses made his decision. On the throne, with his crown upon his head and the slaves holding a canopy over him and fanning him with their bejeweled fans, sits Pharaoh. All about him are the high ministers of state and the lords and nobles of Egypt. Down either side of the audience chamber rigid soldiers, grasping their shields and lances, stand at attention. The porphyry columns of the palace are wound about with serpents and crowned with fierce birds, their eyes and talons flashing with jewels. Pillars burst into flowers, and fountains climb the ladder of the sun. Here, too, is the beautiful princess, the daughter of Pharaoh, all her maids in waiting with her.

Moses, now of age, is summoned before the throne. Pharaoh says to him, "Moses, the end of my life draws nigh. I have no son to reign after me. I am well pleased with you. You have been trained in all the science and lore of Egypt. But you are a Hebrew. If you will renounce your people and be called the son of Pharaoh's daughter, then, when I am gone, all Egypt shall be yours, and you shall sit upon my throne." Silence reigns in the hall as everyone waits for the answer of Moses. His answer, clear and distinct and final, is "No!" He utters one of the sublime no's of the Bible. "By faith Moses, when he was come to years, refused to be called the son of Pharaoh's daughter; choosing rather to suffer affliction with the season; esteeming the reproach of Christ greater riches than the treasures in Egypt."

Suppose Moses had made the other choice. Suppose he had said to Pharaoh on that day, "Yes, I will renounce my people, the despised shepherds from Canaan! Henceforth, I will be the son of Pharaoh's daughter." If that had been his answer, then today some professor of archaeology and Egyptology, lecturing to his classes, would be saying: "The Pharaoh who reigned about the year 1300 B.C., was Ramses II. He was followed by a Pharaoh who was called Moses. The mummy of Moses was discovered in the tombs under one of the pyramids and now reposes in the British Museum in London!" Such would have been the history and the power of Moses had he chosen Egypt instead of Israel and the pleasures of sin instead of the kingdom of God. But because he refused to be called the son of Pharaoh's daughter, because in that hour of trial he believed in the great promises concerning the future of Israel, given to his ancestor Abraham, and because "he endured, as seeing him who is invisible," the name of Moses endures forever. No pyramid could entomb him!

Moses soon acted upon his choice. One day he saw an Egyptian smiting a Hebrew. That is what every age has seen. Always someone smiting the Jew—Assyria, Babylon, Egypt, Rome, Spain, Russia, and Germany. But those who smite the Jew write their own epitaph. Those who know the Bible and know its great promises and warnings concerning the Jew had no doubt from the very beginning as to the issue of World War II. The wicked plot of Hitler against the people of God was sufficient evidence of his eventual overthrow. In the thunder of the bombs that burst over Germany, in the crash of the shells of the artillery, what did one hear? One heard the echo of that word spoken to Abraham ages ago, "I will bless them that bless thee, and curse him that curseth thee."

For his patriotic act in killing the Egyptian who had smitten the Hebrews, Moses had to flee into the wilderness. There he had the great trial of forty years of waiting. After his conversion, Paul had to wait ten years before Barnabas brought him down to Antioch and started him on his great work as an apostle to the Gentiles. But Moses had to wait forty years in the desert before his call came. Here, again, we have another element in the making of the great man and the great voice—solitude. Like John the Baptist, Moses was in the desert until the call of God came. After he had heard the voice at the burning bush, Moses walked by the sound of that voice and by the light of that flame. Not for Moses alone burned that sacred bush. If the history of every life that has been true to God and served its day and generation could be told, it would be discovered that in each life there was a time when through some sorrow or trial or suffering the sacred light burned, and one heard clearly and distinctly the voice of God and henceforth walked in obedience to that voice.

THE FINAL TRIAL OF MOSES

The work of Moses was done. His magnificent life had won for him that great title "Moses, the servant of the Lord." Never once, at the time of the plagues, the Passover, the Red Sea, the rock in the wilderness, the thunders of Sinai, had Moses faltered or failed. Now the goal was in sight. Under his inspired leadership the people were encamped on the banks of the Jordan. Over there, on the other side of the river, was the land of Canaan, the land of promise.

As he stood surveying that promised land, the goal of all his prayers and toils, Moses recalled the warning that he had received after he had smitten the rock twice instead of once and, angrily denouncing the people, had said, "Hear now, ye rebels; must we fetch you water out of this rock?" Because he had not honored God that day in the presence of the people, God told him that he could not go with the people into the land of promise. To us the offense of Moses on that day seems a much less serious offense than when, coming down from the mount and seeing the people dancing about the golden calf that they had made there in his absence, in his anger he flung the Tables of the Law and the Ten Commandments upon the ground and broke them into fragments. But our ways are not God's ways.

Remembering what God had said, Moses pleaded with God to revoke that sentence: "O Lord God, thou hast begun to shew thy servant thy greatness, and thy mighty hand: . . . I pray thee, let me go over, and see the good land that is beyond Jordan, that goodly mountain, and Lebanon." But God said to Moses, "Speak no more unto me of this matter. Get thee up into the top of Pisgah, and lift up thine eyes westward, and northward, and southward, and eastward, and behold it with thine eyes: for thou shalt not go over this Jordan." There Moses stood on Pisgah, the highest peak of Nebo. He could look down upon the encampment of Israel and see the tribes in orderly array about the ark of the covenant with their standards waving in the morning wind. He could see the Jordan, at that time overflowing all its banks, and beyond the Jordan, the fortress of Jericho. To the south was the Dead Sea; to the north, the Sea of Galilee and Mount Hermon crowned with snow. Away in the distance was the rocky eminence, the Hill of Zion, upon which the city of David would one day rise. How the soul of Moses yearned for that land! "I pray thee, let me go over, and see the good land that is beyond the Jordan." But God said no. "Behold it with thine eyes: for thou shalt not go over." And there on Nebo's lonely mountain God buried Moses.

Nebo and Pisgah were not the last mountains upon which Moses was destined to stand. Thirteen hundred years have passed, and Moses again appears upon a mountain. But this time it is in the land of promise on the Mount of Transfiguration.

He died in the hour of his disappointment, but now he has a far grander privilege than that of crossing with Israel's host the river Jordan and standing on the soil of the promised land; for now we behold him appearing in glory with Elijah as the first fruits of them that slept, and speaking with the Son of God concerning "his decease which he should accomplish at Jerusalem." Thus an overwhelming disappointment ended in a glorious destiny.

The history of Moses, in that respect, is repeated in many a faithful life. There is a certain sense in which all of us at the end of life stand on Nebo's lonely mountain. The Promised Land has not been reached. The highest hopes and desires have not yet been fulfilled. To all of us in this life the final word is, "Thou shalt not go over." For all of us it must be written as it was concerning the believers of that ancient day, "These all died in faith, not having received the promises, but having seen them afar off." For all of us God prepares that "better thing," that "better country." This is the way to look upon your sorrows, your limitations, your disappointments. God who is faithful will deal with you as He did with Moses.

> O lonely grave in Moab's land,
> O dark Beth-Peor's hill;
> Speak to these curious hearts of ours
> And teach them to be still.

6

THE TRIAL OF DAVID

The sweet psalmist of Israel (2 Sam. 23:1).

There was no little stir in the hamlet of Bethlehem when, one day, the great prophet Samuel appeared in the town driving a heifer before him as if for a sacrifice. The elders of the town waited upon Samuel and asked him if he came in peace. They feared that his presence in Bethlehem meant that he was the herald of a divine judgment upon the people for some transgression Reassured by the answer that he came peaceably and to offer a sacrifice, they went with him to the house of Jesse where he offered a sacrifice and sanctified that household.

Once again Samuel was on the lookout for a king. The Divine Voice had directed him to the house of Jesse. Jesse had eight sons, the oldest of whom was Eliab, a man of great stature and imposing presence, but imperious and ill-natured. The youngest son was not called at all. He was about fourteen years of age at that time, and probably Jesse did not think that Samuel would give him a moment's consideration in connection with whatever mysterious purpose brought him to his house. When the seven sons were marshaled before Samuel and he looked upon the imposing Eliab, Samuel said to himself, "Surely the Lord's anointed is before him." But the Divine Voice indicated to Samuel that this was not he. "Man looketh on the outward appearance, but the Lord looketh on the heart." Then came Abinadab, and after him

Shammah, who also were rejected; and one by one all the sons of Jesse but the youngest. Then the perplexed Samuel said to the father, "Are here all thy children?" And he said, "There remaineth yet the youngest, and, behold, he keepeth the sheep." "Send and fetch him," said Samuel.

Then came David with his auburn locks and his friendly, attractive face, his boyish form, and perhaps a harp in one hand, his shepherd's staff in the other, and his sling over his shoulder. The moment he looked upon David, Samuel knew that this was he, and anointed him with the oil. Now David, your carefree shepherd's life, roaming over the hills and valleys, keeping watch over the flocks, counting the stars by night, playing to yourself and to your sheep on your harp, dreaming of what the future holds in store for you—all that is past. Your trial, David, a trial that will last for sixty years, has commenced. It is a trial which will bring you many a dark day and many a starless night, a trial which will wring from your lips many a cry of anguish, but a trial which, when it is over, will leave thee forever and ever a blessing to the sons of men and to the church of the living God.

There are men who are great in their character and great in their achievements, but you would not rate them as great personalities. In the Bible there are three who were not only great in their achievements, but were great personalities, ever fascinating and engaging. These are Peter, Paul, and David. David was great in many ways as a poet, musician, warrior, king, and administrator. He was great too as a planner and builder. Yet ever back of it all was his fascinating personality. All Israel loved David. Saul loved him, when he was not possessed with the demon of jealousy; Jonathan loved him and stripped himself for him; his soldiers loved him, and the Lord loved him.

We know more about David than we know about any other man in the Bible. His biography is by all odds the longest in the Bible. Fourteen chapters are devoted to Abraham and eleven to Jacob; but sixty-two chapters in the Old Testament tell the story of David. We know him not only through these narratives, but also in the psalms, where his soul speaks, and the souls of believers of all ages. As a lad David had been brought to the court of Saul to play on his harp and lift the gloom from the soul of the king from whom the spirit of the Lord had departed and to drive out the evil spirit which haunted him. That service of David, his minstrelsy at the court of Saul, was prophetic of his minstrelsy through the ages. By the music of his psalms he drives out from the hearts of men the evil spirits of passion, gloom, melancholy, anger, fear, and doubt.

David's trial follows the trial of Saul. Saul was the greatest failure in the Old Testament. He first was put on trial as king over God's people. He had many great and admirable qualities—courage, magnanimity, humility, and affection. But he never surrendered his will to the purpose of God, and for that reason he was rejected as king over Israel. After that rejection, and the anointing of David, Saul's history is a tragic story of jealousy and murderous and violent rage, with now and then pathetic tears of sorrow and remorse, like gleams of sunlight on a stormy day. At length the end came for Saul on Gilboa's bloody slopes, where he fell on his own sword, the greatest shipwreck of the Old Testament.

It is sometimes asked how it could be that David was called by the Lord "a man after his own heart," when his life was stained with great sins and crimes. The answer is not difficult to give. The first time he was so called was before he had been anointed king, when God told Samuel that he had chosen a man after His own heart who would do His will. There the future kingship of David was contrasted with the reign of willful and disobedient Saul. The second time the Bible speaks of David as a man after God's heart is ages afterward, when the wicked Jeroboam had made Israel to sin. The prophet Ahijah, pronouncing God's judgment upon Jeroboam, contrasts his reign with that of David, "who kept my commandments, and who followed me with all his heart, to do that only which was right in mine eyes." In contrast with these two kings, Saul and Jeroboam, David's long reign was righteous and godly. When he is called a man after God's own heart the reference is not to his personal character, but to the character of his reign. At the same time, as we shall see, there were many things in the life of David which were pleasing to God and which are an example to you and me.

DAVID'S TRIAL IN YOUTH

All men, if they live long enough, are certain to be tried by sickness, the passing of friends, loneliness, and other hardships incident to age. But David was a man who was tried not only in middle life and in his old age but in his youth.

Here he is suddenly turned from a shepherd into a king. The oil of consecration is upon his brow; but as yet there is no crown, no scepter, no throne. He is still just a keeper of sheep. So from the very beginning the faith of David is tried, and he must follow Moses of old who "endured, as seeing him who is invisible." Like all men, David had unconscious preparation and trial for future usefulness. His encounters with the lion and the bear tested him and fitted him for the encounters which were to come. One day his great opportunity came when he chanced to visit the army at that hour of the day when the huge Goliath came forth to blaspheme the God of Israel and challenge the army of Saul. After that notable victory the severity of David's trial commenced.

At the very beginning of these severe trials God granted David one great compensation—the wonderful friendship with Jonathan. Until Jonathan fell by the side of Saul on the battlefield of Gilboa, his friendship was a well of refreshment and encouragement to David; and long after Jonathan's death, too, the memory of that faithful friend touched his heart and moved him to gracious deeds "for Jonathan's sake." Once, in this period when David was being hunted like a partridge on the hills by the furious Saul, insane with jealousy and mad with the knowledge that God had rejected him, and when David was at the very bottom of the pit of despair, this noble friend Jonathan at the risk of his own life came over from the camp of Saul in the dead of night, there in the wilderness of Ziph, and "strengthened his hand in God" and convinced him anew that God's word would not fail and that he would yet be king. Men can endure great trials if they have the guiding and warming lamp of affection and friendship.

On two occasions, David had Saul in his hand and might have destroyed him, once when he cut his robe as he slept in the cave of Engedi and again when he came upon him sleeping in his camp in the tangled forests of Ziph. There you can see Saul sleeping within the trench, his men-at-arms in careless slumber about him, his great spear stuck in the ground near his head. As they look upon Saul lying there in the moonlight helpless before them, Joab's nephew, Abishai, begs permission to seize that spear and slay him. To the ordinary conscience that would appear legitimate, for Saul was seeking the life of David. Just one blow of that spear, and David's trials, so far as Saul is concerned, would be over. But he puts the temptation from him, and says, "The Lord shall smite him; or his day shall come to die; or he shall descend into battle, and perish. The Lord forbid that I should stretch forth mine hand against the Lord's anointed." David waits on providence and follows providence, but he will not force providence He will not seize the throne through assassination.

DAVID'S LATER TRIALS

At length the day came when the long feud between David and Saul was over. Now David was king, first for a few years at Hebron and then at Jerusalem, of which he was the founder and which is well named "the city of David." The sudden elevation to power did not change the natural generosity and magnanimity of David. Saul's death is lamented in one of the great odes of all times, and the men who honored the bones of Saul are recognized and rewarded. Far from taking vengeance on the house of Saul, David inquires if there is anyone left of it, that he "may shew him kindness for Jonathan's sake."

Now we come to the dark day in David's life. For some years he had had prosperity, success, and good fortune. That may be as severe a trial as adversity. David's fall came when he was in the sunshine of power and fame and fortune. One look at the beautiful woman washing herself on the housetop, and David was plunged into the pit. For all time his fall makes him a beacon light of warning.

"Let him that thinketh he standeth take heed lest he fall." The beauty of Bathsheba was a temptation to David, and in that respect a trial for him. And so also was his sin and fall a trial. How men will act after they have yielded to temptation, after they have been wounded and sifted by Satan—that is the supreme trial. Thus David is immortal for his repentance.

God waited long for David to repent, and we cannot imagine that a man who had lived so near to God and delighted in the divine companionship was anything but unhappy and disturbed after his gross transgressions of adultery, murder, and hypocrisy. But still he did not repent. It was at this time that the natural generosity and magnanimity of David gave way to unwonted cruelty and ferocity, when he subjected his enemies in the war against Moab to terrible and cruel vengeance. Then God sent the prophet, the preacher; and Nathan came with that sublime and touching sermon about the rich man who slew the poor man's lamb for the guest who had come to visit him. It was like Hamlet's play within the play, only in this instance the guilty conscience at first was not aroused. But David's fierce anger is not against himself, but against a man who has been so cruel as this hypothetical man of Nathan's parable. Then Nathan told him who the man was—"Thou art the man!"

Now what does David do? Defy the prophet of God? Take off his head, as other Oriental monarchs would have done? No. Instead of that he repents, and of his sincere repentance there is no doubt. "I acknowledge my transgressions: and my sin is ever before me. Against thee, thee only, have I sinned, and done this evil in thy sight." David was forgiven as soon as he had repented. That is always true. There is no wait, no pause, in the outgoing of God's love and mercy and forgiveness when we confess our sins. "If we confess our sins, he is faithful and just to forgive us." If David is a beacon light on the headlands, on the shores of the sea of time, warning all men against temptation and sin, so he is a welcoming and cheering light at the harbor of heaven, calling men to repentance and to return to God.

David had been forgiven; but his sin had been so great, both as an individual and as a ruler of God's people, and had given such occasion, then and ever since, to the enemies of God to rejoice, that the temporal judgments of God must show to all men His displeasure with what David had done. "But the thing

that David had done displeased the Lord." Now we see David
in the trial of retribution.

> Sorrow tracketh wrong
> As echo follows song;
> On! On! On!

That dread "On! On! On!" you see now in the subsequent
history of David. "The sword," Nathan had told him, "shall
never depart from thine house." Now watch the flashing of
that sword! First, the child of sin—who lived so short a time,
but long enough to twine himself around the heart of the royal
father and sinner—was smitten in death. Paul in one of his
letters gives striking utterance to the truth of retribution, that
the way of the transgressor is hard, and also to the added truth
that men are oftentimes punished in the way in which they
themselves have sinned. He says, "He that doeth wrong shall
receive for the wrong which he hath done: and there is no
respect of persons." Literally it reads, "He that doeth wrong
shall receive for the wrong which he hath done."[1] So it was
with David. Sensuality and murder had stained his life and his
reign; and by sensuality and murder David himself is now punished, and punished in his own household. The sword of retribution flashes, and his beautiful daughter Tamar is defiled by
her own brother Amnon. The sword flashes again, and Amnon
is murdered by his brother Absalom. Yet again the sword
flashes, and Absalom rebels against his father and drives him
from his throne. So much did David feel that he was being
punished for his sins, and punished in the way that he himself
had sinned, that when Shimei cursed him as he fled the capital,
and one of David's officers wanted to cut off the reviler's head,
David said, "Let him alone, and let him curse; for the Lord
hath bidden him."

At length came the fearful climax of David's sorrow and
David's trial, when the runner from the battle in the wood of
Ephraim brought the tidings that Absalom had fallen in the
battle; and David went up to the chamber over the gate and as

---

1. Colossians 3:25.

he went thus he said: "O my son Absalom! my son, my son Absalom! would God I had died for thee, O Absalom, my son, my son!" In the surges of that incomparable grief what you hear is not only the sorrow of a loving father over a beloved son, and not only the sorrow of a loving father over a wicked son for whom now there was no hope, but the sorrow of a loving father who loved God and saw in the death of his son his own sin coming back to him.

In David's pathetic grief and unwithdrawn affection for his wicked son, we have, too, as it were, a picture of the love of God for the sinner. The Jews have a tradition that every time that David uttered the cry, "O Absalom, my son, my son!" one of the sevenfold gates of hell opened, until at length the soul of Absalom was admitted to paradise. That tradition was a reaching out after the great truth of the Atonement. David's pathetic plea and his deep love for Absalom could do nothing for him, but the love of God in Christ can reclaim the sinner. At every cry of Christ on the cross one of the gates of condemnation swings open and the soul of the penitent and redeemed sinner is admitted into paradise.

At length comes the sunset and the quiet of the eventide for David. The eye of his genius is not dimmed and his spiritual force is not abated, for at the very last he sings his great psalm of thanksgiving to God. At the end of all his trials, this is his verdict: "As for God, his way is perfect . . . thy gentleness hath made me great." That was his way of saying, what Paul said ages later, "All things work together for good to them that love God."

7

THE TRIAL OF ELIJAH

What doest thou here, Elijah? (1 Kings 19:9).

Elijah, like John the Baptist, is one of the greatest men of the Bible, and one of the loneliest. Except for a brief period at the end of his life when Elisha was with him, we never see Elijah in the company of other men. He had no companions, no fellow worker, none to cheer or encourage him. Only twice in his history do we behold him in any close human relationship—once with the widow of Zarephath who entertained him, and once with Elisha. Like the great prophet who was to come, Elijah trod the wine press alone.

Elijah comes upon the stage of Israel's history like a flash of lightning. Great men are the inspired text of the book we call history. Elijah illustrates the power of a great personality. Strong personalities are mighty, either for good or for evil. World War II illustrated that fact. It was folly to dismiss Hitler, who inspired and unified a depressed, broken, and defeated nation and made that nation a curse, a menace to the whole world, and a fountain of measureless woe, as a "paper hanger." No "paper hanger" could have done that! But thank God, great personalities are mighty also on the side of good. Lone-handed, save for the word of the Lord, Elijah worked a national revolution and turned a whole nation back to God.

Jesus said that no man greater than John the Baptist had been born. The measurement for John was Elijah, for Jesus said that John did his work in the spirit and power of Elijah. The highest tribute paid to Elijah is that when Christ appeared on earth and spoke His parables and sermons and judgments and did his healing works, there were those who took him to be Elijah. In the wilderness of Caesarea Philippi, Jesus asked His disciples, "Whom do men say that I, the Son of man, am?" And they said, "Some say that thou art John the Baptist; some, Elias [that is, Elijah]; and others, Jeremias, or one of the prophets." If Christ made men think of Elijah, then it is well for us to remember that Christ is not all tenderness and benevolence and patience. He, too, like Elijah, spoke scorching words of judgment and retribution. Of all the heroes of the Old Testament, the two who were chosen to appear in glory on the Mount of Transfiguration and speak with Jesus concerning "his decease which he should accomplish at Jerusalem," the triumph of his atonement, were Moses and Elijah. If on the Mount of Transfiguration Jesus found it profitable to speak with Elijah, it will not be without profit for us to look for a little at this magnificent character.

ELIJAH AND THE DROUGHT

It was a time of great apostasy in Israel. Urged on by his heathen wife Jezebel, daughter of the king of the Sidonians, worshipers of Baal, Ahab the king had led the nation down the dark and wicked path of idolatry. There were groves of Baal all over the land and temples of Baal at Jezreel and Samaria. The worship of Jehovah had been all but overthrown in the land. The prophets of God, such as survived, persecuted and harried, had fled and were hiding in the dens and caves of the hills. In the history of Israel we see what is always going on in human history, the effort of the false and the corrupt to defile and pollute the true and the divine. Standing at the historic point in Pittsburgh, where the Allegheny and the Monongahela mingle their floods to form the Ohio, one can see distinctly the flow of the two rivers for a considerable distance after they have formed the Ohio. The Allegheny comes into the Ohio comparatively clear and unpolluted, but the Monongahela is dark and discolored from the mines and factories which are on its banks. Gradually the clearer water of the Allegheny is discolored by the dark waters of the Monongahela. So "evil communications corrupt good manners." So the stream of unbelief and of evil ever seeks to taint and pollute the stream of truth and righteousness. That goes on, not only in the world and human society, but in the church itself. The result is that today, under the name of Christianity, we have two religions which have little in common. One is a religion of reform, of ideals, of ethics; the other a religion of redemption, of regeneration, and of salvation.

Elijah made a sudden and dramatic appearance in the troubled court of Ahab. Standing before the king, he said, "As the Lord God of Israel liveth, before whom I stand, there shall not be dew nor rain these years, but according to my words." Imagine what America would be like, green and pleasant America, if the rains ceased; and still more, what Palestine, a comparatively rainless country, would be like if the rains fell no more. Having delivered his sentence of judgment and coming drought, Elijah vanished into solitude. A price was set on his head. Everywhere the agents of Ahab and Jezebel hunted for the man who had brought such a calamity upon the land. But God had hidden Elijah in the remote valley of the brook Cherith, where he drank of the brook and was fed by the ravens. The purpose of this was not only to protect him from the malice of Ahab, but to prepare him for his future work by teaching him absolute dependence upon God. And what could teach him that so well as to be fed by the ravens?

When the brook at length failed, Elijah crossed the country to Tyre and Sidon on the seashore, where he was sustained by the widow of Zarephath. How strange the providences of God are! Here is this poor widow, who, when Elijah came to her door and asked her for bread, cried out in despair that she was gathering two sticks to make a fire to cook the last handful of meal in her barrel that she and her son might eat it and then die. Yet this is the woman God chose to support and sustain the prophet. How true it is that "God hath chosen the weak things of the world, to confound the things which are mighty."

THE TRIAL BY FIRE

Three and a half years had passed. Elijah was sent to meet Ahab and pronounce the end of the drought. When he met the king he told him to assemble all the prophets of Baal, four hundred and fifty of them, and all the people on the slopes of Mount Carmel. Never was there such an assembly since Joshua assembled the people together between Mount Ebal and Mount Gerizim and called upon them to choose that day whom they would serve—the God of Israel or the heathen gods that their fathers had served on the other side of the flood.

The view from Mount Carmel is one of the most interesting and stirring in all the Holy Land. Out to the west is the Mediterranean; to the north Ptolemais, or the modern Acre, and the road to Tyre and Sidon; to the east Kishon, once choked with the bodies of Sisera's soldiers, and later to be choked again with the carcasses of the slain prophets of Baal. Still further to the east, the Valley of Esdraelon, the battlefield of Gideon and the Midianites, and towering over the plain, Mount Tabor. This was the setting for the trial by fire. Elijah challenged the people, "How long halt ye between two opinions? If the Lord be God, follow him: but if Baal, then follow him." This was one of the decisive moments in the history of Israel.

> Once to every man and nation
>   Comes the moment to decide,
> In the strife of truth with falsehood,
>   For the good or evil side.

Such an hour had come for Israel. When Elijah made his challenge, the people answered him not a word. Their silence would seem to announce their rejection of Baal and their purpose to follow the Lord God of Israel.

At the direction of Elijah, the prophets of Baal built an altar, and having slain a bullock, cut it in pieces and laid it on the wood of the altar, but put no fire under the altar. Elijah then announced that the priests of Baal would invoke their god and then he would invoke the God of Israel. "The God that answereth by fire," he said, "let him be God." To this the people all agreed. When they had dressed their altar, the priests of Baal circled and danced about it from early morning until noon, shouting, "O Baal, hear us!" But there was no voice and no fire to answer them. In their despair they leaped upon their altar and, crying aloud, cut themselves with knives and lances until the blood from their wounds poured down in a crimson stream upon the altar. And all the while Elijah derided them and mocked them, "Cry aloud; for he is a god!" He must be in conversation with some other God, he told them; or perhaps he is out hunting, or it may be that he has gone on a long journey, or perchance he is taking an afternoon nap and must be awakened. All afternoon the prophets of Baal kept up their shouting and their dancing. But now the shadows were beginning to fall over the mountain, and Baal had not answered.

Elijah now summoned the people to come near to him. Taking twelve stones, one for each of the twelve tribes of Israel, Elijah repaired one of the broken-down altars that had been abandoned during the reign of wicked Ahab and Jezebel. Then he dug a trench about the altar, and, having slain the bullock and placed it upon the wood, he had the attendants pour the contents of four barrels of water on the sacrifice and on the wood, so that what was to follow would be all the more wonderful. Three times they poured the water upon the sacrifice and upon the wood of the altar, until the water filled the trench around the altar.

Now had come the time for the offering of the evening sacrifice, a sacrifice long neglected in Israel. Elijah lifted up his voice in prayer and said, "Hear me, O Lord, hear me; that this people may know that thou art the Lord God, and that thou hast turned their heart back again." Then the fire of the Lord fell from heaven and consumed the sacrifice and the wood and the stones and the very dust and licked up the water that was in the trench. When the people saw what had happened, they fell on their faces and said, "The Lord, he is the God; the Lord, he is the God."

The Lord had answered from heaven by fire, but not yet had the rain come. After the prophets of Baal had been slain, Elijah told Ahab to eat and drink for the rain was coming.

Then Elijah went himself to the top of Carmel and cast himself down upon the earth and, putting his face between his knees, told his servant to go off on the promontory and look toward the sea. Six times the servant did this, while Elijah wrestled in prayer, and six times he came back with the announcement, "There is nothing." But when he went the seventh time he said, "Behold, there ariseth a little cloud out of the sea, like a man's hand." Soon there was the roll of thunder and the flash of lightning. The heavens were black with cloud and wind, and there was a great rain. Elijah, girding his loins about him, ran like a conqueror before the chariot of Ahab to the palace at Jezreel. What a picture that is of the triumphant Elijah! He is the very incarnation of victory and triumph as he runs before that chariot!

THE TRIAL IN THE DESERT

There was at least one person in Israel who was not impressed by Elijah's victory on Mount Carmel. When Jezebel heard what had happened to her prophets, in a paroxysm of rage she said, "So let the gods do to me, and more also, if I make not thy life as the life of one of them by tomorrow about this time." Now we see Elijah running once more. But this time it was not in triumph in front of the chariot of Ahab. This time he fled before the burning chariot of Jezebel's wrath and vengeance. Far into the desert he fled, and, falling down at length beneath a juniper tree, he cried out to God, "It is enough; now, O Lord, take away my life; for I am not better than my fathers." He had thought he had succeeded where they had failed in overthrowing idolatry. But now the queen of the idolaters herself had compelled him to flee for his life. What a contrast we have here! The Elijah who in the past had thundered, "As the Lord God of Israel liveth, before whom I stand," now prostrate beneath the juniper tree, pleading for death!

God knows how to deal gently with his discouraged servants. First of all came the angel who gave him food and drink, and then came sleep, "sleep that knits up the ravell'd sleave of care, . . . balm of hurt minds." After the sound slumber, Elijah was awakened and having refreshed himself again, set out on a journey of forty days and forty nights into the wilderness of Sinai, and there at Horeb, where God had given the law to Israel, Elijah took refuge in a cave. Standing at the mouth of the cave, Elijah heard the voice of God. "What doest thou here, Elijah?" Elijah was quick to justify himself and explain why he was there. He said, "I have been very jealous for the Lord God of hosts: for the children of Israel have forsaken thy covenant, thrown down thine altars, and slain thy prophets with the sword: and I, even I only, am left; and they seek my life, to take it away." The answer of God was the still small voice: "The Lord passed by, and a great and strong wind rent the mountains, and brake in pieces the rocks before the Lord; but the Lord was not in the wind: and after the wind an earthquake; but the Lord was not in the earthquake: and after the earthquake a fire; but the Lord was not in the fire: and after the fire, a still small voice."

The Lord had passed by. Elijah had what he needed, a new vision of God. He was reassured, first of all, as to the state of religion in Israel. God was a better counter than Elijah. Elijah had counted just one worshiper of the true God left, and that one himself. But God told him that there were at least seven thousand who had not bowed the knee to Baal or kissed him. After all, Elijah was not so lonely as he thought he was. The next step in the restoration of Elijah was a new commission. God put him to work again. His commission was to go to Damascus, where he was to anoint Hazael to be king over Syria, and then into Israel to anoint Jehu to be king over Israel, and after that he was to choose Elisha to be his successor.

Soon the great life and ministry of Elijah came to an end. His trial was over, and "nothing in his life became him like the leaving it." What a magnificent scene that is! Elijah, accompanied by Elisha, smiting with his garments the waters of the Jordan as they cross over. Elisha's prayer for a double portion of Elijah's spirit. Then the whirlwind and the chariot and horses of fire. Gazing up into heaven as Elijah was translated, Elisha cried out, "My father, my father! the chariot of Israel, and the horsemen thereof."

The trial of Elijah was a trial of discouragement and disappointment. James said that Elijah was a man of like passions with us, and although he was so mighty and effectual in prayer he was never more a man of like passions with us than in his juniper hour of discouragement and disappointment. We have our personal discouragements, such as are due to long sickness or overwhelming sorrow or the frustration of our plans and hopes. The Devil, according to the legend, once advertised his tools for sale at public auction. When the prospective buyers assembled, there was one oddly shaped tool which was labeled "Not for sale." Asked to explain why this was, the Devil answered, "I can spare my other tools, but I cannot spare this one. It is the most useful implement that I have. It is called 'Discouragement,' and with it I can work my way into hearts otherwise inaccessible. When I get this tool into a man's heart, the way is open to plant anything there I may desire." The legend embodies sober truth. Discouragement is a dangerous state of mind because it leaves one open to the assault of the enemies of the soul.

When moods come upon us, we are apt to take mistaken views of others and of the world and sometimes of God Himself. At such a time it is well to remember that old saying:

> Come what come may,
> Time and the hour runs through the roughest day.

God has His tender ministry for us in these hours of discouragement and disappointment.

> Judge not the Lord by feeble sense,
> But trust him for his grace.

But there is a still deeper disappointment. It is the discouragement that comes from considering God's cause in the world and the part that we can play in it. When he sat there beneath the juniper tree, Elijah felt that he had accomplished nothing and that the worship of Baal would now be triumphant. All his labors, he thought, had gone for nothing. The same discouragements have been felt by other great souls: by Jeremiah, who wanted to flee from his people to a lodging place in the wilderness; by John the Baptist, who sent out of the dungeon that message of doubt to Jesus, "Art thou he that should come? or look we for another?" by brave John Knox, who said at the end, "The world is weary of me, and so am I of it."

There are conditions in the world which are of a nature to discourage men. In national affairs, the spread of the liquor habit, the mounting of divorces, the increase in crime, the ebb tide in religious worship; in international affairs, the recognition that a league of nations for peace must be armed to enforce peace, in other words, peace by the sword; in the Christian church, its slow growth, the flood of worldliness, the little sacrifice or denial, the invasion of unbelief—all this is of a nature to make a man, if he forgets the power of God, lose heart and cry out, "It is enough! now . . . take away my life." The remedy for such an hour and for such a thing is, first of all, the assurance that God gave to Elijah that He has not forsaken His cause, that He never leaves Himself without a witness, that always there is that mystical, invisible, indestructible company of seven thousand who have not bowed the knee to Baal.

> Workman of God! O lose not heart,
>   But learn what God is like;
> And in the darkest battlefield
>   Thou shalt know where to strike.
>
> Thrice blest is he to whom is given
>   The instinct that can tell
> That God is on the field, when He
>   Is most invisible.

The next step in our cure is to return to our work and to remember that our work, however humble it may seem, is necessary and important. Suppose that in the day of Nehemiah, when they were building again the ruined and fallen walls of Jerusalem, those workmen had asked themselves, "In so vast an undertaking, in the midst of such wholesale devastation and ruin, what will the work of my trowel or my hammer amount to?" Yet each man did his work on his part of the wall, and the walls of Jerusalem rose again. The best cure for doubt or discouragement as to the cause of righteousness and Christ's cause in the world is to go to work, and as we work, let us fasten our eyes upon him, of whom the prophet said of old, "He shall not fail nor be discouraged, till he have set judgment in the earth."

8

THE TRIAL OF DANIEL

Thou shalt rest, and stand in thy lot at the end of the days (Dan. 12:13).

The grandest object upon which the sun looks down today is a man of high moral character. Crimson autumn forest, towering mountain, vast ocean, endless desert—these are nothing in majesty compared with a man of noble character. He need not be a famous man, but if he is a man of high moral principles, and stands true to them, come what may, he is the most majestic, the most influential and the most inspiring force in the universe.

When God, through the prophet Ezekiel, was pronouncing the coming doom and judgment upon apostate Jerusalem, as a sign of the certainty of its doom and the irrevocableness of the decree of judgment, he said: "Though Noah, Daniel, and Job, were in it, . . . they shall but deliver their own souls by their righteousness." In other words, Daniel is mentioned as one of the three men in Old Testament history, up to that time, whose reputation and influence were the greatest and who, if any, could have saved Jerusalem from its fate. The influence of Daniel has been greater with young men, I suppose, because of his moral courage and his stand for right, than that of any other character in the Bible, with the possible exception of Joseph. From age to age he inspires young men. If more young men would imitate Daniel, there would be fewer wrecks upon the shores of time. Some of the characters of the Bible instruct us not only by their virtues, but by their sins and their repentance. Among these are Noah, Jacob, David, Solomon, and Peter. But Daniel instructs us by his virtues and by his resistance to temptation and sin.

THE FIRST TRIAL

Daniel was one of the four young Hebrews selected out of the captives from Jerusalem to be educated for the public service at Babylon. They were young men of splendid physique, alert mind, good disposition, and spirit. You can imagine how they felt when for the first time the huge tawny capital of Babylon loomed up over the horizon. The city stood upon a flat plain and was built in the form of a square, fourteen miles on each side. The massive wall was higher than most temples and so broad that many chariots could drive abreast on top of it. In the fifty miles circumference of the city there were one hundred gates of bronze, and two hundred towers rose over the walls. Through the midst of the city flowed the river Euphrates. Here were palaces and temples higher than the pyramids of Egypt. Here were the hanging gardens, with their flowers and forests and fountains, which Nebuchadnezzar had built for his queen, homesick for the hill country whence she had come.

Here, then, in this splendid capital of Babylon was the stage of Daniel's trial. During World War II the Soviet government issued a proclamation to its soldiers as its armies began to invade other lands, exhorting them to be loyal to the principles and fashions of Soviet Russia and not to follow the customs or adopt the ideas of the lands and kingdoms which they were invading. That is very often the result and sequence. Young men are caught with the styles and fashions of a world different from what they have been accustomed to, and, unless they have strength of character, they take on the color of their new environment. They are like the chameleon, which adopts the coloring of whatever its body happens to lie against—leaf or branch or stone or earth. Alas, how many chameleon Christians there are

The first thing which confronted Daniel and his companions was an invitation to sit at the king's table. This meant that they must drink wine that had been offered to idols and eat things which were forbidden to the faithful Hebrew. It was this invitation which precipitated the crisis and trial in Daniel's young manhood. What should he do? What would others have done under those circumstances? Some might have decided upon a week's delay before making their decision. From what they did afterward, when they were confronted with their own great trial, there is no good reason to think that Shadrach, Meshach, and Abednego would have suggested any such compromise to Daniel; but for the sake of making the situation clear, let us imagine these three young men with Daniel in their chambers getting ready for dinner and discussing the invitation from the king.

Let us suppose that Shadrach said, "I think it would be unwise peremptorily to decline this invitation. Let us go along for a week or two, and then, when we have won the good will of the king's chamberlain, we can let him know about our scruples, and then perhaps he will permit us to have another menu." If they had yielded to that proposal they would have been lost, so far as their stand for principle was concerned. Nothing is more fatal to the right stand than a delay in taking it. Satan has won half his battle when he persuades a soul to postpone a decision as to moral principles. Again, let us suppose that Meshach said, "After all, true religion is not what we eat or drink, but the thoughts we think and the deeds we do and the life we live. What difference will it make whether we eat swine's flesh or not, or drink wine offered to the idols?" And let us suppose that Abednego said, "We might as well consent, for we are far from Jerusalem, and there is none to observe us or to know whether we have been faithful or not to the customs of the Jewish people. Our future career is in Babylon. Jerusalem is ended. We must plan our life for this new environment. It would be foolish to prejudice our interests by taking a peculiar stand as to what we eat and drink. It would subject us to ridicule and might possibly result in our being dismissed from the king's court. Our great opportunity would be gone, and we would probably have to toil as slaves in the kitchens or in the brick yards. We are in Babylon now. Let us do as the Babylonians do!"

But none of these considerations, whether suggested by Daniel's companions or not, moved him in the least. "Daniel purposed in his heart that he would not defile himself." He uttered one of the great no's of history. Plutarch wrote of a city whose inhabitants became slaves to others because they could not pronounce the word "no." The inability to say No has made many a young man the slave of the world and its appetite. If I were asked to name a weapon to be put into the hands of a young man or a young woman, which, courageously used by them, would best defend them from the perils and temptations of the world, I would say, Let that weapon be a ringing, courageous, uncompromising no! How many lives have been stained, how many hearts broken, how many bright prospects blasted, for the lack of a no like that of Daniel. The old hymn "Have Courage, My Boy, to Say No!" with its ringing chorus, has a world of truth in it:

In courage, my boy, lies your safety,
  When you the long journey begin;
Your trust in a heavenly Father
  Will keep you unspotted from sin.
Temptations will go on increasing,
  As streams from a rivulet flow;
But if you'd be true to your manhood,
  Have courage, my boy, to say No!

What was the result of Daniel's stand? The result was that he was promoted to great honor. He won the respect instead of the scorn and ridicule of those in authority. This is a corrupt, wicked, and fallen world; and yet even such a world in its heart of hearts has high respect for the man who takes a stand for principle. When Salmon P. Chase, starting as a young lawyer in Cincinnati, made a speech one day in opposition to slavery, one of the ablest lawyers of that bar remarked to another lawyer, "There's a bright and promising young man; but he has ruined his career by the sentiments which he has just expressed." It turned out, however, to be the very opposite, for the young unknown lawyer became governor of Ohio, United States senator, one of the chief founders of the new party of freedom, and under Abraham Lincoln the great Secretary of the Treasury.

What was the secret of the victory of Daniel and his friends? Although no mention of it is made here, I am sure that what he did, as we know in other crises which arose, he must have done here; that is, he strengthened himself by prayer. Daniel made an *immediate* decision. Had he parleyed or postponed, he would have been lost. But when he received that invitation, he raised the flag of his principles immediately so that no one could misunderstand where he stood. That is the way to deal with temptation. That is the way Christ dealt with temptation when He entered into no debate with Satan but said, "It is written," and then, finally, "Get thee behind me, Satan!"

Again, Daniel had prepared himself before the actual temptation came. I imagine on the long journey on the way down to Babylon Daniel had been saying to himself, "In this world I shall be confronted by strong temptations to depart from God and from the way of my fathers. I must, therefore, be strong and resist them at the very beginning." Thus it was that when the temptation came Daniel knew just what he would do. He had "purposed in his heart that he would not defile himself." That phrase, "would not defile himself," is a great suggestion and inspiration for young men and young women. "Know ye not that your body is the temple of the Holy Spirit which is in you, . . . for ye are bought with a price: therefore, glorify God in your body." It was John Milton who said that he kept himself clean from the defilements and dissipations in which his fellow students at Christ College indulged because he had a "just and pious reverence for my own person." In another great passage he wrote that there were two considerations which ought to keep a man from sin: one, that he had been created in the divine image; the other, that he had been redeemed by the precious blood of Christ.

THE SECOND TRIAL OF DANIEL

Daniel was now the aged statesman. Four successive kings found that Daniel, a man of such high moral character, such courage, and such ability, Hebrew though he was, was indispensable for the administration of the empire. Daniel had served under Nebuchadnezzar. It took courage for him to interpret Nebuchadnezzar's dreams and tell him that he would be driven out from his kingdom to eat grass like oxen, that his body would be wet with the dew of heaven, that his hair would grow like eagle's feathers and his nails like birds' claws until he had learned "that the heavens do rule." But fearlessly Daniel gave him the interpretation. Again, under Belshazzar, when the hand came forth and wrote on the banquet house wall, before the terrified Belshazzar and his drunken lords and concubines, Daniel did not shrink from telling him the doom that the hand had written.

Now Daniel is prime minister under the third ruler, Darius the Mede. Because of his preeminence and his ability, Daniel is the object of envy to the pagan princes and statesmen. "Wrath is cruel, and anger is outrageous; but who is able to stand before envy?" Daniel's enemies are determined to bring him down. But how to do it? That is the question.

I can imagine a conference among these conspirators. One of them says, "Let us 'frame' Daniel. Let us forge letters and bring them to the king, stating that Daniel has been in treasonable correspondence with foreign princes and that he plans to rebel against Darius and overthrow his dynasty." But one of the others answers: "No, there is no use in trying that. Daniel has served too long and too loyally under three kings, Nebuchadnezzar, Belshazzar, and now Darius, for anyone to believe such a charge against him as that." Then another makes this suggestion: "Daniel has charge of the finances of the realm. Let us charge him with peculation and dishonesty." But another answers, "That, too, will be in vain. No charge against the honesty of Daniel, who has handled the funds of three kingdoms, will be entertained for a moment. In all these reigns Daniel has been found faithful; neither was there any error or fault found in him." Then the third conspirator comes forward with his suggestion: "There is only one plan that will work." "What is that?" ask the others. "We must devise some plan," says he, "by which Daniel's loyalty to the king will be brought into collision with his loyalty to God." "Yes," say the others. "But how can we do that?" "This," he answers, "is the way we will do it. Listen! Do you hear the roar of the lions? This we will do. We will persuade Darius to sign a decree to the effect that for thirty days no prayer shall be made to any man or to any God save Darius. That will do the business; for if there is anything that is certain, it is that Daniel will never obey such a decree."

The others all agree that this is the best plan. Off they go to the court, and, telling the king that there is some risk of disloyalty in the realm, and also playing on his vanity, they persuade Darius to issue the decree. If anyone violates it, if anyone prays to any man or to any god but Darius for thirty days, he shall be cast into the den of lions. The decree is written, stamped with the king's signet ring and soon posted all over the city and in a conspicuous place around the palace of Daniel where he is sure to see it. Then the next day at dawn, the plotters secrete themselves in the gardens around Daniel's house and wait to see what will happen.

They know that every morning, every noon, and every evening, it is the custom of Daniel to come to his window, the window opening toward Jerusalem, and, opening it, to pray to the God of the Hebrews. Now the long night is past. The sun begins to touch with life and beauty the Euphrates River, the hanging gardens of Nebuchadnezzar, the brown palaces of Nebuchadnezzar, and the hundred gates of bronze in the great walls which surround the city. But still Daniel's casement is not opened. The plotters begin to fear that their plan has failed. "Who would have thought," one asks the others, "that the old man would lose his courage now and cease to pray? He has heard the music of the lions' roar on the other side of the wall, yonder, and that has been too much for him." But before the others can answer, the aged statesman comes to the window, kneels down, spreads out his hands toward Jerusalem, and lifts up his voice in prayer to the God of Abraham, Isaac, and Jacob. That one act clothes Daniel with immortality. As long as the river of time flows, streams of beneficent influence shall flow from the life of Daniel. Come, Caesar! Come, Alexander the Great! Come, Napoleon! Come, all you conquerors of history, and bow down before this man who is greater than you all!

Daniel might have said on that occasion: "I will stop pray-ing for just thirty days. For almost three times a day for thirty years I have prayed openly to God. Now, since my life is at stake, I am sure God will pardon me if for just thirty days I stop praying." Again, he might have said, "I will not stop pray-ing, but I will pray in my own chamber." But that was not what Daniel said or did. He opened his window, as he had been wont to do, so that all his enemies and the king and the whole world and the ages to come might see him and hear him pray.

After a sleepless night the troubled king hurried to the den of lions, and standing at the mouth of the den called down into it, "O Daniel, servant of the living God, is thy God, whom thou servest continually, able to deliver thee from the lions?" And back from the bottom of the den came Daniel's answer: "My God hath sent his angel, and hath shut the lions' mouths, that they have not hurt me." Then was Daniel taken out of the den and promoted to new honor and glory. The story might have had another ending. It might have pleased God to let the lions devour Daniel. But that would have made no difference in the grandeur of Daniel's stand. Delivered though he was, to all intents and purposes Daniel had offered up his life for his conscience, his principles, his God. And greater courage, greater fidelity, has no man than this, that a man should lay down his life for his own soul.

Great honor is bestowed upon Daniel—honor by his king, and honor by God. "The secret of the Lord is with them that fear him." For Daniel, as perhaps for no other personality of the Old Testament, the curtain of the future is lifted. "The eyes of the Lord run to and fro throughout the whole earth, to show himself strong in behalf of them whose heart is perfect toward him." Daniel, the "man greatly beloved," is permitted to behold the vast and thrilling cyclorama of world history—kingdoms rising and falling and disappearing, strange conquer-ors trampling other conquerors down; the ram with the two horns, the rough stamping goat, the beast like a bear, the beast like a leopard with wings, the beast like a lion, and the beast with iron teeth which devoured and stamped the residue in pieces. He saw earthly thrones cast down, and the Ancient of days upon his throne. At the end of these overwhelming visions, Daniel fainted. He was astonished at the visions, and yet could not fully understand it (which is true to a degree of those who read his prophecy today). But he was given the great assurance that his own place in human history and his lot in the kingdom of God is forever secure. The voice of God said to him, "Go thy way till the end be: for thou shalt rest, and stand in thy lot at the end of the days." And there, then, we leave Daniel standing in his lot, with the light of heaven shining upon his face. We commit him to that glory and future happiness in those words which he himself spoke: "And they that be wise shall shine as the brightness of the firmament; and they that turn many to righteousness, as the stars for ever and ever."

9

THE TRIAL OF EZEKIEL

At even my wife died: and I did in the morning as
I was commanded (Ezek. 24:18).

"The Lord is there!" That is the way the book of Ezekiel
comes to a close. That is the impression that it leaves on
one's mind, after all its visions of glory, its predictions of battles
and slaughters, its soaring eloquence, its strange symbols, its
extraordinary dramas—"The Lord is there!" And that is the
impression, too, which the great book leaves about the prophet
Ezekiel, that God was with him, and in his message. Any book,
prophet, preacher, providence, experience in life that can say
that to you, that can tell you that life is more than meat and
the body more than raiment, that can persuade you that life
has spiritual outgoings, and that the destiny of the soul is
something more than just a struggle in the darkness in the
defiles of this world's wilderness, after which silence and noth-
ingness—any book, any friend that can say to you "The Lord
is there" is well worthy of your attention and your gratitude.

Ezekiel is one of the major prophets, and there is no doubt
about his right to that title. He is one of those "dead, but
sceptered sovereigns"—real sovereigns of the world—"who still
rule our spirits from their urns." He had been taken a captive
down into Babylon some years before the final destruction of
Jerusalem by Nebuchadnezzar. He was a contemporary of
Jeremiah, who remained in Jerusalem to the end, and probably

had heard Jeremiah preach at the temple. Ezekiel lived with the captives on the banks of the river Chebar, a hundred miles or more up the Euphrates from Babylon. There he shared with them their sorrows and their exile. Like another great deliverer, he was "touched with the feeling of our infirmities." He says of them, "I sat where they sat." It was then that there came to him the series of extraordinary visions which are related in his book, and it was there he acted out those extraordinary dramas, messages of judgment in pictures which were to fall upon the apostate city. The book concludes with a vision of a temple as large as Jerusalem itself and of a city as large as Palestine, with the temple in the midst of it, and of city and of temple it is written "The Lord is there." So it shall be written of the ideal commonwealth, the kingdom of redemption, when Christ shall have delivered over His mediatorial kingdom to God, and God shall be all and in all.

Although one of the greatest of the prophets, and his book one of the greatest, Ezekiel is sometimes enigmatic and very difficult. He overwhelms you and dazzles you with his acted-out tableaux, such as lying on his side for months at a time before a miniature model of Jerusalem, representing the siege of the city. He awes you with those stupendous visions such as the amber cloud, out of which emerge the four living creatures accompanied by four wheels, high and dreadful, and their rings full of eyes. You follow him with dread into the valley of dry bones and stand in awe when the bones come together with a great shaking and stand upon their feet, an exceeding great army. You stand aghast at that great battle where Gog and his army are overcome, the dead so numerous that it takes seven months to accomplish their burial. Thus it is, that of all the prophets, Ezekiel seems the most remote from our life and thought and understanding.

But there is one exception to this. It is the brief autobiographical passage with which we have to deal here. In it we discover that Ezekiel after all is a man of like passions with you and me. Here is that "one touch of nature" which "makes the whole world kin."

In the midst of his prophetic labors Ezekiel receives a strange and solemn message. The word of the Lord came to him saying:

"Son of man, behold, I take away from thee the desire of thine eyes with a stroke: yet neither shalt thou mourn nor weep, neither shall thy tears run down." Ezekiel refers to his wife as the "desire of his eyes. Evidently this was no formal or merely legal association. His young wife was the desire, literally, the delight, of his eyes. She must have been the kind of wife described by that master of English style, Jeremy Taylor: "Her voice his sweet music; her smile his brightest day; her kiss the guardian of his innocence; her arms the pale of his safety, the balm of his health, the balsam of his life; her lips his faithful counselors; her bosom the softest pillow of his cares; and her prayers the ageless advocates of heaven's blessing on his head."

His wife, Ezekiel is informed, will be taken from him by a stroke. "I take away from thee the desire of thine eyes with a stroke." In the domestic blow which fell upon him Ezekiel is to recognize the hand of God. That is always true; whether it is a child who dies before its lips have learned to form a single word or the nonagenarian tottering on his staff or the young man cut down in the strength and beauty of his youth on the battlefield—always it is God's stroke and God's will. And in that fact and reflection is the refuge, and the only refuge, for your soul.

To Ezekiel the blow must have been overwhelming, and yet he is not permitted to give any token of grief or sorrow. He is not to put on the customary habiliments of mourning. He is not to lament or cry aloud; he is not to seek the comfort of his friends and his fellow men in his great grief but is to go on about his high task as a prophet as if nothing had happened. When the people, amazed at this seeming hardness of heart and indifference on the part of one whose sympathetic and affectionate nature they well knew, asked him what he meant by such strange conduct, he was to tell them that it was a picture and prediction of their own state of mind when the final judgment should fall upon apostate Jerusalem. Those judgments would be so terrible, and the destruction of the city so complete, that the survivors would be so dazed and overwhelmed that they could not give expression to the usual tokens of sorrow. Their anguish would find no relief in outward expression, in those tears which are the safety valves of the heart.

It is not, however, the symbolic significance of what
Ezekiel did that interests us and grips us today, but the
splendid heroism of it. "At even," he said, "my wife died.
And I did in the morning as was commanded." That is all
that Ezekiel tells us about it. But in your imagination you
can fill in the blank pages of that autobiography. "I did in
the morning as I was commanded." But he says nothing of
what took place that night between the last ray of the sinking sun and the first beams of the morning sun: the tumult
of emotion, the vain appeals, the voiceless lips of the
unreplying dead, the groping hands stretched through the
night, the lonely vigil by the side of the beloved dead, the
trusting of the larger hope—all this there is not an intimation, not an echo. But in the morning you see him standing
girded for his prophetic task, master of himself, master of
his grief, obedient to God. "I did in the morning as was
commanded."

This incident is a lofty example of the subordination of
private grief to public duty and service. Ezekiel certainly was
moved; he certainly suffered, but he realized that his nation
and his message were more important than the vicissitudes of
his personal life. He drowned his sorrows in the sorrows of his
city and his people.

PRIVATE SORROW AND PUBLIC DUTY

In our own history we have an example of this subordination of private grief to public duty in the life of the man of
sorrows who occupied the White House during the Civil War.
His heart was lightened and his sorrows alleviated by the pranks
and rompings of his two younger sons, William and Thomas,
who with their Western ways and independence kept the White
House in joyous uproar. But early in February, 1862, Willie
sickened and died. It was the President's greatest personal sorrow. He went on with his public duties; but, like the king of
Samaria, he wore sackcloth within. Here and there we have a
suggestion of what he was passing through. Once on a warship
at Fortress Monroe he picked up a copy of *King John* and read
that beautiful passage where Constance expresses the fear that

she will not know her son, the imprisoned Arthur, when she meets him in the life to come.

> And, father cardinal, I have heard you say
> That we shall see and know our friends in heaven:
> If that be true, I shall see my boy again;
> For since the birth of Cain, the first male child,
> To him that did but yesterday suspire,
> There was not such a gracious creature born.
> But now will canker sorrow eat my bud
> And chase the native beauty from his cheek
> And he will look as hollow as a ghost,
> As dim and meagre as an ague's fit,
> And so he'll die; and, rising so again,
> When I shall meet him in the court of heaven
> I shall not know him.

When he had finished the reading, he turned to his aide and said, "Did you ever dream of a lost friend and feel that you were holding sweet communion with that friend, and yet have a sad consciousness that it was not a reality? Just so I dream of my son." And with that he bowed his head upon the desk and surrendered himself to his grief. But the nation saw nothing of that struggle. Messages had to be sent to the Congress. Senators and congressmen had to be interviewed, defeated generals encouraged, incompetent ones replaced, armies and fleets dispatched, and the heart of the nation strengthened in the Lord. His own private sorrow was subordinated to public duty and to the sorrows of the nation.

In another great personality of that same period we see the same devotion to public duty. In October, 1863, after the great campaigns on the Mississippi, General Sherman, accompanying his family up the river, stopped at Memphis. There his son William, a lad of nine years, sickened and died. Sherman sent the child's body on with the mother and a group of officers to their Ohio home and with a heavy heart turned back to the command of his army. In a letter written the day after the boy's death, Sherman said:

The child that bore my name, and in whose future I reposed with more confidence than I did in my own plan of life, now floats a mere corpse, seeking a grave in a distant land, with a weeping mother, brother, and sisters clustered about him. For myself, I ask no sympathy. On, on I must go to meet a soldier's fate, or live to see our country rise superior to all factions till its flag is adored and respected by ourselves and by all the powers of the earth. God only knows why he should die thus young. He is dead, but will not be forgotten till those who knew him in life follow him to that same mysterious end.

In the evening his son died, but in the morning he did as he was commanded.

One of the great stories of reform is that of the struggles of Richard Cobden, the Manchester industrialist, and John Bright, the Rochedale spinner. They were not content just to make money and succeed in life in the business sense. They looked upon the masses of Great Britain, caught in the chains of industrial slavery, and were moved with compassion. They met first in the chapel of a Baptist church at Rochedale, where Bright had asked Cobden to come and speak in the interests of the education of children of workers. But it is doubtful if John Bright had ever become the colaborer and disciple of Cobden in the work of reform had it not been for the sorrow that crushed his early hopes, and the wise ministry of his friend Cobden in that critical hour.

Bright had written Cobden, informing him of the death of his young wife:

It has pleased the Almighty to take from me my beloved and cherished companion. She sank peacefully to her rest about one o'clock this day. She had almost no suffering, and death to her had long lost his terrors. Until she became mine, I did not know that mortality ever was the abode of so much that was pure and lovely. Her sainted spirit, I cannot doubt, is now an inhabitant of that city "where none can say he is sick," and in this deep affliction my heart rejoices in the full assurance that to my precious wife the change is inconceivably glorious. I know thou wilt sympathize with me in this very deep trial and it is therefore I write to inform thee of it. I hope this may reach thee before thou leaves tomorrow.

In his speech at the unveiling of the Cobden statue at Bradford in 1877, Bright told the story of Cobden's response to his letter:

> At that time I was at Leamington, and on the day when Mr. Cobden called upon me—for he happened to be there at the time on a visit to some relative—I was in the depths of grief, I might almost say of despair, for the light and sunshine of my house had been extinguished. All that was left on earth of my young wife, except the memory of a sainted life, and a too brief happiness, was lying still and cold in the chamber above us. Mr. Cobden called upon me as his friend and addressed me, as you might suppose, with words of condolence. After a time he looked up and said, "There are thousands of houses in England at this moment, where wives, mothers, and children are dying of hunger. Now," he said, "when the first paroxysm of your grief is past, I would advise you to come with me, and we will never rest till the Corn Law is repealed."
>
> I accepted his invitation. And since then, though there has been suffering, and much suffering, in many homes in England, yet no wife and no mother and no little child has been starved to death as the result of a famine made by law.

In the evening Bright's wife died, but in the morning he did as God commanded, and millions of people blessed his name because he subordinated private sorrow to public duty.

PRIVATE SORROW AND PRIVATE LIFE

We are not in places of public trust as Ezekiel was, or leaders in public life and action like those whose names I have just mentioned, yet we come face to face with the same kind of trial, and our victory, if it is won, must be won along the same lines as those on which Ezekiel won his victory, when in the evening his wife died, and in the morning he did as God commanded. Think of the thousands of fathers and mothers and wives and children and brothers and sisters who in the great war received the intelligence that the "desire of their eyes" had been taken away by the stroke of battle. You read in the paper the brief dispatch sent by the late General Patch, commander of the Seventh Army in France, informing his wife of the death in action of their only son. It read: "Mac killed instantly today in an attack upon an enemy position." That was all; but that was enough; and down in Virginia the iron entered into a woman's soul. Yet the general in command had to leave the body of his son in its quickly dug grave. So men and women stricken in their hearts must go on and do their duty in the battle of life.

Last summer I visited the Hall of Fame at New York University. There, overlooking the Harlem, and with the noble Palisades of the Hudson in the distance, I looked on the busts of the seventy-three famous Americans chosen thus far, from George Washington to Pittsburgh's Stephen Foster. Under the bust of each of these famous men is some suitable inscription, generally a statement by the famous man himself. Under the bust of Robert E. Lee is this word: "Duty is the sublimest word in our language."

Whatever happens in life, duty always remains. In the expression of private grief there is always the risk of selfishness. It was for that that the gruff and somewhat unfeeling but wise and loyal Joab rebuked David after the great battle in the wood of Ephraim, where Absalom had fallen. In the paroxysm of his sorrow, David forgot for a moment his kingdom and the welfare of the state. When the soldiers heard of the king's grief, their own rejoicing was turned into mourning, and they stole away to their tents as if ashamed. It was then that Joab came to David and told him that by his untempered grief he cast a reflection upon the gallantry and sacrifices of the soldiers who had jeopardized their lives in the forefront of the hottest battle for him and for his kingdom. When David heard that, he came to himself and arose and sat in the gate and saluted and thanked his army.

No matter how heavy the heart is, duty always remains. That is the grand thing about these prophets of the Old Testament: their loyalty to God and duty at all cost, with disregard for their personal comfort and welfare. A singular thing about these prophets—you never hear of their death. You hear of the deaths of the patriarchs, Abraham, Isaac, and Jacob, and the deaths of the kings, Solomon and Saul and David and Josiah. But rarely do you hear of the death of the prophets. The death of Moses was kept secret; Elijah was taken up into heaven with a whirlwind; but of the death of Isaiah and Jeremiah and Jonah and Ezekiel you hear nothing. Figuratively speaking, they never die, as if to show that their message is timeless and dateless. In their loyalty to God they are beyond the limitations of time. Heroic souls, they thought only of the flaming light they carried. The lamp must burn, the light must shine, the word must be spoken.

What Ezekiel did when he conquered his private grief in his devotion to God and duty was done through faith. We are not speaking of iron resolve, of the endurance of a stoic, but of the faith of a Christian, the faith of a Paul, who said, "I can do all things through Christ which strengtheneth me." It is through that faith that the morning always comes and duty can always be done. Our faith is the faith of the morning. "Weeping may endure for a night, but joy cometh in the morning." And after all the struggles and battles and trials of this life comes at length the light of the eternal morning, when in His light we shall see light,

> And with the morn, those angel faces smile
> Which I have loved long since, and lost awhile.

10

THE TRIAL OF PETER

Thou shalt be called Cephas, which is by
interpretation, a stone (John 1:42).

The trial of your faith (1 Peter 1:7).

That is the story of the trial of Peter: how Christ transformed a man of clay into a stone. The geologist tells us that much of the rock that now forms the surface of the earth was once clay. So every human soul has in it the capacity, under divine grace, to become a redeemed soul, to become a character and personality upon whom men can build.

One of the joys of heaven to which we can look forward with the greatest expectation will be the joy of seeing and meeting and hearing the great personalities of the Bible: Abraham, Joseph, Moses, Elijah, Daniel, David, Isaiah, Jeremiah, Jonah, John, Barnabas, Paul, and Peter. I imagine, too, that the one that we shall have the least difficulty in recognizing will be Peter. He is the one of the apostles about whom we know the most. He spoke more, asked more questions, uttered more exclamations and ejaculations than all the others; and more than all the others, too, he was instructed, exhorted, reprimanded, warned, and blessed by Christ. Not only what Peter said, but what he did, and the way in which he did it, makes him a man who reveals himself and is easily identified. Such a character as Peter could never have been invented or counterfeited. Any of the other apostles would have looked foolish and sounded foolish if he had tried to talk like Peter or act like Peter.

Peter is the man of impulse and of quick action following those impulses. For that reason he appears sometimes as a man who contradicts himself. Some of his actions and some of his words are in striking contrast with others. So he has been described as a man who is "consistently inconsistent." He salutes Jesus as the Son of God, and the next moment tries to give advice to the Son of God and receives a severe reprimand from Jesus. When he heard Jesus say, that night on the stormy sea of Galilee, "It is I; be not afraid!" immediately all his fear left him, and he tried to walk to Jesus on the water. But the next moment he was sinking and crying out in despair, "Lord, save me!" At the Last Supper he protested that Jesus would never wash his feet, and then the next moment he asked Jesus to wash not only his feet but his head and his hands. With splendid boldness, he drew his sword and smote the servant of the high priest; but within another hour he quailed before the pointed finger of a servant girl and denied that he had ever known his Lord.

Even after the Resurrection and the Ascension, Peter shows lingering traces of that variableness, impulsiveness, and inconsistency. It was he who through the vision which was granted him on the housetop at Joppa preached the Gospel to the Roman centurion, Cornelius, and thus opened the gates of the kingdom to the Gentiles. And yet it was the same Peter, who, after he had fraternized with the Grecian converts at Antioch, when followers of James, the brother of the Lord and the head of the strict Jewish party, had come down to Antioch, withdrew himself from their fellowship and refused to eat with them, and had to be withstood and rebuked by Paul. Yet, through it all, the great impulses of Peter are on the side of Christ and on the side of righteousness. Sometimes the wind shifts; but the prevailing winds that sweep over the sea of his life are Godward.

In the study of Judas we shall see that he had the greatest of all trials. Called to be an apostle of the Son of God, a founder of the church of the living God upon earth, in that highest trial he made the greatest failure of history. Peter, likewise, had the highest of all trials, called to be an apostle of the Son of God; and in that trial he won the greatest of all victories, achieved the highest success, not only because with the other ten he was found worthy to be an apostle, but because he won the victory in spite of one sad and terrible failure and transgression. That is why I rank Peter in his trial as the greatest moral success of all history.

The best way to describe Peter and his trial is not to analyze him in a cold, logical way, but to let Peter describe himself and tell his own story in his own words and in his own dramatic and never to be forgotten actions.

What is the first time that we hear Peter speak? It is that morning by the Sea of Galilee when Jesus, walking along the shore of the sea, saw two boats drawn up on the shore and four fishermen near them washing their nets. He selected one of the boats, that which belonged to Andrew and Peter, and, when he had asked them to push out a little from the beach, taught the multitude out of the boat. Then he said to Peter, "Launch out into the deep, and let down your nets." Peter said, "Master, we have toiled all the night, and have taken nothing: nevertheless, at thy word I will let down the net." Immediately they made such a haul of fish that the net was likely to break, and they had to halloo to their partners, John and James, to row over and help them land the fish.

Then what did Peter do? What is the first religious expression we have out of his mouth? It is this: falling down at his Master's feet there in the boat, among the nets and the fishes, Peter cried out, "Depart from me; for I am a sinful man, O Lord." In this, almost his first, meeting with Christ, Peter knew and confessed himself to be a sinful man. That is the first fact of Christian faith—"I am a sinful man." This first fact of Christian experience will also be the last fact of Christian experience, for we are told that all the music of the life to come will be the music of those who knew and confessed that they were sinners but now are no longer sinners because their sins have been washed from them in his own blood. The conviction of sin, the sense of your need in the presence of Christ— that is the key that opens the door to all the chambers and all the treasures of the Christian life. Begin there, where Peter began, and you are on the road to final victory.

Take the next great utterance of Peter. In the desert country around Caesarea Philippi Jesus asked His disciples, "Whom do men say that I, the Son of man, am?" In answer they gave him the popular report or supposition. Some thought He was mighty Elijah come back to earth, according to the prediction of Malachi; some thought He was the great Jeremiah, and some that He was one of the prophets, but which one they were not certain. Then Jesus pressed His disciples to give their own opinion, "But whom say ye that I am?" Then Peter broke out with his great answer, "Thou art the Christ, the Son of the living God." Jesus blessed him for that confession and told him that it was given him by an inspiration of heaven, that flesh and blood had not revealed it to him, and that upon that rock—the truth expressed in Peter's confession of the divine sonship of Christ—his church would be so firmly built that the gates of hell could not prevail against it. It was a divine inspiration, and yet it is significant that it was to Peter, who already had given expression to his great need of being saved from his sins, to whom this great answer was given. There was something in Peter's make-up, in his thought and aspiration, in his relation to Jesus, which made it fitting and proper that he, of all the apostles, should be the one who should make that great confession. There, again, Peter's words and Peter's convictions constituted a rock upon which Christian faith was to be built. First, that we are sinners—"Depart from me"—and second, that we have a mighty Savior who is the eternal Son of God. The blunder that Peter made immediately afterward, in trying to hold Christ back from the great act of sacrifice for sin upon the cross, must not dim the grandeur and preeminence of his confession.

This brings us to another great utterance of Peter. About the same time as that great confession, Jesus had made it clear that His kingdom was not of this world. After He had fed the multitude with the loaves and the fishes, they were about to take Him by force and make Him a king. But Jesus refused that worldly honor and withdrew Himself from them. He also made clear the difficult terms of discipleship, and John tells us that about "that time many of the disciples went back, and walked no more with him." Perhaps it was as He saw some of them going off that Jesus turned to the twelve and said, "Will ye also go away?" Then again Peter gave the great answer, "Lord, to whom shall we go? thou hast the words of eternal life."

To Peter thus fell the distinction of being the first to give expression to the preeminence of Christ and the indispensableness of His love and His power. Christ is not *one* of the leaders, *one* of the saviors of mankind, but "there is none other name under heaven given among men, whereby we must be saved." When Peter said that, when he was preaching to the high priest and the officers at Jerusalem, after he and John had been imprisoned, he was but rephrasing what he had said on this memorable occasion to Jesus, "Lord, to whom shall we go? thou hast the words of eternal life." How indispensable to you is Christ? Is there any other one to whom you go, or any other place you seek, for the abiding satisfactions of life?

We come now to another great moment in Peter's trial and training and to another great utterance. It is often dealt with as though it were an index to a fundamental weakness in Peter's character. But that is a profound mistake. It is an index to his strength. After He had fed the multitude and dismissed them, Jesus sent the disciples across the sea in their ship while He Himself went alone into the mountain to pray. While He was praying in the mountain a storm broke on the Sea of Galilee, one of those sudden convulsions for which that usually so placid body of water is notorious. At the fourth watch of the morning, the dark hour just before the dawn, the disciples, toiling at the rowing, thinking that they were going to perish, and that Jesus perhaps had forgotten them, saw what they took to be a ghost striding toward them on the crest of the waves. They could battle against the storm, but a ghost, a water demon, that was too much for them, and they cried out in terror. Then they heard the voice that they knew and loved so well, "Be of good cheer; it is I; be not afraid."

The moment Peter heard that voice all his fears were gone, and he cried out, "Lord, if it be thou, bid me come unto thee on the water." "Come," said Jesus. "And when Peter was come

down out of the ship, he walked on the water, to go to Jesus."
That is the part of the narrative that most people forget. They
remember only that Peter sank when he became frightened,
and cried out, "Lord, save me!" But for a little Peter did walk
on the water, and Jesus encouraged him to do so. He was
pleased with Peter's venture of faith. He is always pleased
when He sees us ready to try great things and to venture all
our faith in Him. Over the angry sea of life's sorrows and
troubles and dangers Christ bids us come to Him, and as long
as we look to Him and trust in Him, we can walk on that
troubled sea; and when we do forget Him and begin to sink,
we can always make that final prayer of Peter: "Lord, save
me!"

We come now to the final stage of Peter's trial—his temptation and fall. Were it not that we read it here in the inspired
records, we would say it is an incredible thing that a man who
loved Jesus as Peter evidently did, who had been so long in
His fellowship, who understood so well His power and His
grace, should have denied his Lord in the way he did. It is, in a
sense, more astounding than the sin of Judas, for we have no
record of expressions of loyalty or affection from Judas such as
we have on the part of Peter. His fall is all the more astounding, too, because of the solemn, definite, and particular warning that was given him by Jesus. Jesus did not openly tell the
disciples that night who it was that should betray him, but He
did tell them who it was that should deny Him. In the midst of
the supper He turned to Peter and said, "Simon, behold, Satan
hath desired to have you, that he may sift you as wheat: But I
have prayed for thee, that thy faith fail not: and when thou art
converted, strengthen thy brethren." To that warning Peter
responded as we might have expected. "Lord, that is impossible. Thomas might fail You; Philip or Judas, or even John
here, might deny You, but not I!" he said in effect. "Lord, I
am ready to go with thee, both into prison, and to death." And
Peter at that time honestly thought that he was ready. But how
unready he was the sequel soon proved. Jesus said to him,
"Peter, the cock shall not crow this day, before that thou shalt
thrice deny that thou knowest me."

It is very significant that Jesus, when He came from His

agony and found the three disciples sleeping in the Garden of Gethsemane, spoke not to James nor to John, but said to Peter, "Simon, sleepest thou? couldst not thou watch one hour?" It is as if in His human nature Jesus was amazed that Peter had gone to sleep. This is one of the few occasions when Peter is silent. He had nothing to say—nor was that strange. But when he had been roused out of his guilty slumber the third time, Peter was himself again and was ready for action. When he saw his enemies crowding around Jesus, Peter took out that sword he carried and struck a mighty blow at one of them, cutting off the ear of the servant of the high priest. Although Christ rebuked him for his mistaken idea of defending Him, Peter stands out in that incident as a man of splendid courage, ready to fight for his Lord against that whole crowd. It was when he saw Jesus bound and led away that Peter must have had his troubled doubts. Probably, like Judas and the rest of them, he never thought that Jesus would permit Himself to be taken by His enemies. But there He was, bound and buffeted and insulted, and led off into the night by His foes.

"And Peter followed afar off." Many sermons have been preached on that text. But it is well to remember that although he followed him afar off, Peter did better than all the other disciples with the single exception of John, for "they all forsook him, and fled." They did not follow Him at all; but Peter followed Him afar off, never losing sight of Him, wondering in his heart what was going to happen to his Lord.

Peter had been accused several times of being a friend and disciple of Jesus and had vehemently denied it. A relative of the high priest's servant, Malchus, whose ear Peter had cut off, accused him again, saying, "Did not I see thee in the garden with him?" Now thoroughly frightened, Peter sprang to his feet and began "to curse and to swear, saying, I know not the man." Just then two things happened. The cock crowed, and at the same moment the door of the judgment hall opened and Jesus was led out, beaten and bleeding, just in time to hear the curses of His denying disciple. "And the Lord turned, and looked upon Peter."

What a sermon could be preached on the looks of Jesus! The look of anger, that time when He looked around Him upon the people who were watching to see if He would heal that man with the withered arm on the Sabbath day. That look of worship and thanksgiving when, before He distributed the loaves and the fishes, He looked up to heaven and gave thanks. That time when they brought to Him the woman taken in adultery, and looking down He wrote in the dust; and that time when they brought to Him the man that was dumb and deaf, and looking up to heaven He sighed; and that time when the woman with the issue of blood touched the hem of His garment, and Jesus looked around to see who it was that touched Him; and again, when He heard the request of the rich young ruler and, looking upon him, loved him; and again, when He turned, with the mists of death coming over His eyes, and looking upon the dying thief at His side, said, "Today, shalt thou be with me in paradise." And that night at the last supper when He looked up to heaven and began His sublime intercessory prayer. But most wonderful of all was the look that Peter got that night when "the Lord turned, and looked upon Peter."

What was it that made Peter go out and weep bitterly? It was not remorse, or shame, for he must have been feeling that the whole time he sat there about the fire amid the enemies of Christ. Neither was it the memory of the warning of Jesus, now brought to mind by the crowing of the cock. No, it was something else. It was the look of wounded love, the love that still loved him despite his cruel and cowardly lie, the love that would not let him go. In that look was the secret of Peter's victory, for, after all, Peter was victorious that night. His courage had failed him; but his faith, in answer to the prayer of Jesus, had not failed him. And now that wondrous look of Jesus centers the faith of Peter once again upon his Lord.

In the restoration of Peter there were four steps. First of all was that look that Jesus gave him. Then came the special message sent him by the angel of the resurrection, "Go tell his disciples and Peter"—as if the angel thought the women would no longer consider Peter as a disciple and might forget to tell him. The third step was a special appearance of the risen Lord to Peter, for when the two who had walked with Him on the road to Emmaus had returned to the meeting place of the

disciples at Jerusalem, they were greeted with the great tidings, "The Lord is risen indeed, and hath appeared to Simon."
Of all the resurrection appearances of Jesus, that is the one
about which we would like to know the most, but it has pleased
the Holy Spirit to draw over it the veil of silence. But there
was another appearance which the pencil of the Holy Spirit
has recorded for us.

Seven men in a boat, weary and tired and disheartened, after
a whole night of fishing and catching nothing. The boat rising
up and down with the gentle pulsation of the sea. The mists
rising from the lake. Suddenly they hear, these seven men in the
boat, a voice hailing them, "Children, have ye any meat?" When
they had answered "No," John, who has been looking intently
through the mists at the figure on the shore, exclaims to Peter,
"It is the Lord." Overboard without a moment's delay goes
Peter! There you can see him leaving the clumsy boat far behind him and breasting the water with broad and powerful
strokes. And there he is, the water dripping from his garments
as he comes up the beach where Jesus is waiting by the fire.

When they were eating the broiled fish that morning about
the fire, and the seven disciples were all silent, they all knew
that it was Jesus, and yet something made them afraid to speak.
Then Jesus Himself broke the silence. He turned to Peter and
said, "Simon, . . . lovest thou me more than these?" When
Jesus had asked him that three times, Peter was grieved and
said, "Lord, thou knowest all things; thou knowest that I love
thee." There was a new Peter. No longer the impulsive and
boastful Peter, always ready with words, but a new, humble
and chastened Peter. No boasting this time about how he loved
his Master, but simply, "Thou knowest that I love thee."

Now Peter got his reinstatement and his new commission
to feed the flock of Christ. Henceforth, every day of his life,
until they take him and crucify him, Peter would answer that
prayer of Jesus, "When thou art converted, strengthen thy
brethren." In his great trial Peter had come off conqueror and
more than conqueror. Satan had lost and Christ had won.
Satan thought that he surely had him when he heard him curse
there in the court of the high priest. He thought he had him as
surely as he had Judas. But Satan had lost! Christ had won!

We are all on trial. Peter is not the only disciple of Jesus whom Satan desires to have that he may sift him as wheat. And how many ways and devices he has to get hold of men's souls and sift them out of their character and out of their faith! But the victory of Peter is the eternal encouragement for every tried and tempted soul. We may falter at times; we may fall at times as Peter did; but if we have seen that look of Christ, if His love is in our hearts, we shall never fail. We shall, as Peter wrote long afterward in his first letter, be "kept by the power of God through faith unto salvation."

11

THE FIRST TRIAL OF JESUS

Then was Jesus led up of the Spirit into the wilderness,
to be tempted of the devil (Matt. 4:1).

The lights have been extinguished. In the vast limestone cavern where we are standing, far beneath the surface of the earth, the guide tells us to be silent and listen. As we listen in the darkness and in the silence, we can hear far beneath us the flow of an underground river. Races and generations of men have come and gone. Empires and kingdoms have risen and fallen, but still that stream has been flowing on in the darkness, never ceasing, its work never done. So temptation flows like a river through the life of man. How long temptation has been here! How old it is! How unchanging it is! It is as recent as the latest birth and old as death. It touches the lives of the fool and the philosopher, the prince and the pauper, the savage and the sage, of John and Nero, John the Baptist and Herod, Paul and Judas. Temptation is the warfare from which there is no discharge

The last temptation of Jesus was in the Garden of Gethsemane, when He prayed, "If it be possible, let this cup pass from me." Here we are concerned with the first assault of Satan, the first trial of Jesus. Temptation comes at the beginning of His life and then departs from Him "for a season," but only to return at the end. Man's warfare with temptation is not ended until he obtains his crown. Until then it is not safe for him to lay his armor down.

The temptation of Jesus was a natural and inevitable prelude to His work as the Redeemer from sin. On the cross He tasted death for every man, and in the wilderness He tasted temptation for every man. The temptation of Jesus was a lonely experience. Mark, in his account, says He "was with the wild beasts." Temptation is something you cannot share with anyone else. Satan always talks to one man, never to ten men or a thousand or ten thousand. He takes the soul whom he desires to tempt apart into a desert—a lonely place. The scene of your temptation may be a quiet study, a busy thoroughfare, or an unfrequented path through the forest; but always, when Satan comes, the soul is alone.

"Then was Jesus led up of the Spirit into the wilderness, to be tempted of the devil." There you have the answer for those who are troubled about the petition in the Lord's Prayer, "Lead us not into temptation, but deliver us from evil." Does God lead us into temptation? Yes, just as certainly as the Spirit led Jesus into the wilderness to be tempted of the Devil. But that is quite different from leading yourself into the wilderness of temptation, from reading those books and forming those associations which stir and arouse the evil that is within you. But it is the appointment of God that in this world of probation and trial we shall be placed in circumstances where we shall be tempted and where we must choose between good and evil, with all the tremendous issues which flow from such a choice.

THE TEMPTATION OF THE FLESH

The tempter came to Jesus when after forty days of fasting He was "hungered." It would have been no temptation to Jesus in His flesh if the tempter had come after the first or second day, but after the fortieth day it was a great temptation. The famished body must have leaped at the very mention of bread. We need not pause to observe what things, and sometimes what terrible things, men have done under the powerful urge of this elemental appetite, hunger.

The Devil said to Jesus, "If thou be the Son of God, command that these stones be made bread." The desert was strewn, and is strewn, with stones not unlike loaves of bread in shape.

Pointing to them, the tempter said, "If thou be the Son of God, command that these stones be made bread." You must not take that as meaning that Satan is asking for a demonstration and proof of the divine sonship and deity of our Lord, as if he had said to Him, "You claim to be the Son of God. Now prove it by turning these stones into bread, and then I will believe on you." By no means. The one person who has no doubt as to the complete deity of Jesus Christ is Satan. That mighty intellect—for he is a mighty intellect, though fallen from his heavenly estate—knows full well the truth as to Jesus and His divine nature. Doubts as to the deity of Christ he has left to be expressed by the puny intellect of man. When Satan then said, "If thou be the Son of God," it amounted to saying, "Since thou art the Son of God, command that these stones be made bread." Satan is not challenging Jesus to work a great miracle and prove His deity. What he is trying to do is to move Jesus to make use of His miraculous powers to satisfy His hunger and thus depart from the path that God at this time had outlined for Him. Christ was hungry, and hunger is a natural, not a sinful, appetite. On occasions Christ did make use of His miraculous power to preserve His life. But here in the desert He is to obey God's will. To work a miracle to satisfy His hunger was not in keeping with His work as a redeemer. Therefore, Christ said to Satan, "It is written, Man shall not live by bread alone, but by every word that proceedeth out of the mouth of God."

You must live. "Self preservation is the first of all laws." That was what Satan, no doubt, said to the heroic prophet Micaiah. When Jehoshaphat and Ahab inquired of him whether or not they should go up to battle against Ramoth-gilead, all the false prophets, four hundred of them, had said, "Go up . . . for the Lord shall deliver it into the king's hand." But Jehoshaphat was anxious to hear what a true prophet of the Lord would have to say on the matter. The messenger who came to summon Micaiah into the presence of the two kings gave him what he thought was a friendly warning: "Behold now, the words of the prophets declare good unto the king with one mouth: let thy word, I pray thee, be like the word of one of them, and speak that which is good." But to this Micaiah answered, "As the Lord liveth, what the Lord saith unto me, that will I speak." Because of his unfavorable prediction concerning this expedition, Micaiah was cast into the prison and fed with the bread and the water of affliction. But he had been true to God and true to his conscience, and his name lives forever.

"A man must live," the tempter said to John Bunyan when he could have been released from the dungeon, if he had promised to silence his witness for Christ. And Bunyan thought of his wife and children, especially his blind girl Mary, of whom he would say, "O my poor blind one, what sorrows thou art likely to have in this life. How thou must go naked and hungry and beg in the streets and be beaten and starved, and now I cannot so much as endure the thought that the wind should blow upon thee." But Bunyan thought of something else that must live. He thought of his conscience and said, "The moss shall grow upon these eyebrows before I surrender my principles or violate my conscience."

Yes, a man must live. Satan spoke a greater truth than he thought when, by implication, he said that to Jesus, and asked Him to turn stones into bread. A man must live, but that man is not the animal man but the man of conscience, the man of the soul, the man who lives to eternity. That is the man who must live and that man cannot live "by bread alone, but by every word that proceedeth out of the mouth of God."

TEMPTING GOD

Here Satan tempts Jesus to try God by asking for His protection and care in an action not in the path of duty. "Then the devil taketh him up into the holy city and setteth him on a pinnacle of the temple." This pinnacle was one of the turrets of the temple of Herod, rising six hundred feet above the valley of Jehoshaphat. The Devil can tempt a man in the desert and he can tempt him in the church. The temple, the church, was the scene of the second temptation. Standing on the pinnacle of the temple Jesus could survey the whole city. Here for centuries the tribes had gone up; here Judah's kings had reigned and died; here all the rivers of the Old Testament had deposited the golden sands of their inspiration and prediction. What memories must have stirred in the breast of Jesus as He surveyed that scene!

It was at such a moment, with such memories stirring in His breast, that Satan said to Jesus, "If thou be the Son of God, cast thyself down: for it is written, He shall give his angels charge concerning thee; and in their hands they shall bear thee up, lest at any time thou dash thy foot against a stone." Here again, as in the first temptation, Satan is not asking Jesus to prove that He is the Son of God by a divine intervention saving Him from death on the rocks in the valley of Jehoshaphat six hundred feet below. What He is trying to do is to persuade Jesus to test His own divine sonship by throwing Himself from the parapet. If he were rescued from death on the rocks below, His deliverance would dazzle the people of Jerusalem and gain Him recognition at once as the Messiah, without His having to take the path of humiliation and rejection and death. Such a miracle would convince Jerusalem and the high priests, and through them the whole nation, that Jesus was the Son of God.

When Satan said, "If thou be the Son of God, cast thyself down," it amounted to saying, "Since You are the Son of God, you can certainly do this and claim divine protection and rescue, for it is written in the psalm, 'He shall give his angels charge over thee, to keep thee in all thy ways. They shall bear thee up in their hands, lest thou dash thy foot against a stone.'"

The answer of Jesus is taken from Deuteronomy, where we have a reference to the smiting of the rock at Horeb. The complaining and unfaithful people asked, "Is the Lord among us, or not?" Their sin was to question the presence of God with Israel unless they had a miracle to prove it. So when Jesus quotes the commandment from Deuteronomy, "Ye shall not tempt the Lord your God, as ye tempted him at Massah," He means that to cast Himself down from the pinnacle of the temple and count on a miraculous deliverance would be a questioning of God's power and presence in His life.

This second temptation may at first seem remote to our own life, for the trouble with most people is that many have too little faith, not to speak of a faith which would lead them to cast themselves down from a precipice. Nevertheless, there is such a thing as tempting God, that is, in the sense of presumptuously demanding His miraculous intervention. The plan of life for us is that we should walk by faith and not by sight. If we could have a miracle every day, there would be no need for our faith.

Wherever men ask for more signs, more evidence of the truth of the Gospel, of salvation, of the life to come, than God has granted us, there they are tempting, that is, trying, God. Wherever men expect spiritual strength and a happy destiny without a struggle—as Balaam did when he prayed, "Let me die the death of the righteous, and let my last end be like his"—without using the means appointed of God, there they are tempting God. Wherever men go into dangerous places, into the areas of sin and temptation, expecting to be preserved from contamination simply because they bear the name of Christ, there they are tempting the Lord their God. Take the question, too, of the life to come. We have the revelation of the New Testament. We have the resurrection of Christ; we have the great word of Jesus, "Let not your heart be troubled: ye believe in God, believe also in me." To endeavor, then, to peer into future life by the necromancer's rod or by the tripod of the witch of Endor, is to try the Lord our God, because such action shows a lack of faith in Him, His goodness, and His Word.

THE TEMPTATION OF POWER

If we follow the order of the three temptations as we have them in Matthew's Gospel, then the climax was in the third temptation, the temptation of ambition and power.

This time, having been defeated in the other two subtle temptations, Satan casts aside his disguise, both of himself and of the thing that was to be done. What he asked Christ to do in the other two temptations was not, in itself, sinful; but here he casts aside all reserve and boldly asks Christ to do a wicked thing, to worship the Devil and be rewarded with the dominion of the world. In a moment of time he took Him to the top of a high mountain, either actually or in vision, and showed

Him all the splendor of the kingdoms of this world and said, "All these things will I give thee, if thou wilt fall down and worship me."

The power of Satan in this world and in this dispensation is, undoubtedly, very great. He is spoken of as the prince of darkness, the prince of this world, the ruler of the darkness of this world. These titles indicate great temporary power in Satan's hand. The state of the world today, too, certainly indicates such power. Satan must have a certain grim satisfaction when he sees what he has accomplished in the world. In His answer to Satan, Christ does not seem to question his right to offer what he had offered—the kingdoms of this world—but resists the proposal as the worship of Satan instead of the worship of God. "Thou shalt worship the Lord thy God, and him only shall thou serve."

The third temptation was a temptation to the love of power. Christ, indeed, had been promised all the kingdoms of this world. In the second psalm, God says to His Son, "Ask of me, and I shall give thee the heathen for thine inheritance, and the uttermost parts of the earth for thy possession." But now Satan suggests to Jesus that at the price of a momentary prostration before him, He can secure the kingdoms of this world without traveling the hard road of Gethsemane and Calvary.

Satan still promises men great things if they will but fall down and worship him, even for one moment. To many a man he offers the great ends of his ambition if he will but compromise with evil.

To the man in political life Satan makes his proposition: "If you will do this or that—make these appointments, be silent as to this evil—then I will see that you take your seat as governor or senator." That was the temptation to which the great minister of Henry VIII, Cardinal Wolsey, succumbed. When he came to die he said:

> O Cromwell, Cromwell!
> Had I but served my God with half the zeal
> I served my king, he would not in mine age
> Have left me naked to mine enemies.

Naaman, the prime minister of Syria who had been healed of his leprosy by the prophet of God, was generous, grateful, and sincere in his desire to be a worshiper of the true God. But he had high rank under the Syrian king, and one of his duties was to escort that monarch when he went to worship the false god. Would Elisha permit that weakness? "In this thing," said Naaman, "the Lord pardon thy servant, that when my master goeth into the house of Rimmon to worship there, and he leaneth on my hand, and I bow myself in the house of Rimmon; when I bow down myself in the house of Rimmon, the Lord pardon thy servant in this thing." How few there are who can hold their high office without having to pray to some named or unnamed Elisha to pardon them and excuse them for just this one bending of the knee to that which is wrong and dishonorable.

The physician who was called to attend Herod the Great when he lay rigid in one of his moments of remorse and sorrow said:

> To me indeed it seems, who with dim eyes
> Behold this Herod motionless and mute,
> To me it seems that they who grasp the world,
> The kingdom and the power and the glory,
> Must pay with deepest misery of spirit,
> Atoning unto God for a brief brightness,
> And ever ransom, like this rigid king,
> The outward victory with inward loss.[1]

Christ alone, who refused the scepter of the world, was fit to wield it. The world is at the feet of Him who cannot be tempted.

Suppose that Jesus had yielded to Satan's shameful hint! Imagine Him, if you can, dazzled by the phantasmagoria of world empire, and for the sake of that dominion bowing down to Satan! "What shall it profit a man, if he shall gain the whole world, and lose his own soul?" That question, it is important

---

1. Stephen Phillips, *Herod*. Used with permission of John Lane, the Bodley Head, Ltd., London, England.

to note, was asked by the only man who was ever offered the whole world and refused it. Alas, not for the whole world, but for one poor paltry bit of its dust, for one little moment of the world's enjoyment, men sell their souls!

The fact that Satan attacked Jesus is one that ought to solemnize every one of us. If the tempter came to Jesus, then we can be certain he will come to us. If he attacked the Son of God and sought to bend Him to his will, then whom will he not assail? Satan desires to have us, each one of us, that he may sift us as wheat—sift us out of our character, our principles, our honor, our purity, and our faith. But we have a Captain of our salvation who Himself met our great foe and conquered him. He conquered him, not only for Himself and for His own ministry, but for you and me today. If by watching and prayer we keep ourselves in Jesus' company, Satan can do us no harm. "Greater is he that is in you," John said, "than he [that is, the tempter, Satan] that is in the world."

The conclusion of this great drama of temptation is, in certain respects, the most wonderful thing in it. When Jesus said to the tempter, "Get thee hence, Satan," then the Devil "departed from him for a season" and "angels came and ministered unto him." Sacred, blessed, heaven-sent angels! And still they come! Still, poised upon their wings, they wait to see what will be the outcome of our battle with temptation. Anxious and ready they are to come down as of old and minister to him who has not bowed the knee to Satan and who, tempted by this present world, has chosen instead his soul's welfare and eternal life.

When Christian had given Apollyon the mighty thrust and that black demon spread his wings and departed, the Pilgrim sat down on the grass to rest and to dress his wounds. Then there appeared a Hand which had in it the leaves of healing, and these Christian took out of the Hand and applied to his wound. Wounds which have been received in resisting evil can always be healed. A Hand is extended down to touch them with the leaves of the Tree of Life which are for the healing of the soul. The only wounds which cannot be healed are the wounds of infidelity, of cowardice, and of despair. "Then the devil leaveth him, and . . . angels came and ministered unto him." God grant that that may be the end of your battle and my battle with temptation. "Then the devil leaveth him, and . . . angels came and ministered unto him."

12

THE TRIAL OF JOHN MARK

And fled from them naked (Mark 14:52).

John departing from them returned to Jerusalem (Acts 13:13).

Take Mark, and bring him with thee; for he is profitable
to me for the ministry (2 Tim. 4:11).

Three texts! The record of two failures, and one great success and recovery.

Midnight in Jerusalem. In the Passover moonlight the shadow of the temple of Herod falls across the city, and the shadow of the massive walls to the north and the east fall across the gorges above which they rise. In the city all are asleep—all but sickness, sorrow, hate, and guilt. The Supper is ended, the traitor has gone out. Jesus and His disciples, to the music of one of the grand old psalms, have come down from the upper chamber, descended the hillside, crossed the bridge over the Cedron, and made their way into Gethsemane. Even there, all soon are asleep, the eight disciples near the gate, and even the chosen three—Peter, and James, and John. But not Jesus. No. He slept once, while the others were awake, on that pillow in the stern of the boat on stormy Gennesaret; but now, while the others sleep, Jesus is awake.

There are some others, too, who are awake; the scribes and the Pharisees and Judas Iscariot, for "hate is the insomnia of

106

the soul." In the ample house of well-to-do Mary, John Mark, her son, is asleep. Suddenly he awakens, hearing the hurried tramp of feet on the street. At first he thinks it is only a dream. Then he arises and, looking out of the window, hears the murmur of voices and sees the light of torches in the distance. Then he goes back to bed and sleeps. For the second time he awakens, this time with a fear in his heart that perhaps harm is meant to Jesus. Not waiting to dress himself, but clad only in his nightdress, Mark hurries by a shorter route to Gethsemane than that by which the crowd with Judas and the scribes and Pharisees are marching. From the direction which they are taking, he knows that they are headed for Gethsemane, where Jesus is wont to go at night to pray.

Secreting himself in the shadows of the trees of the garden, Mark watches as Jesus is taken captive and led off toward the city. All the disciples by this time have forsaken Him, at least temporarily, and fled. But Mark follows closely after the mob. His white robe attracts the attention of one of the officers, and, accusing him of being a follower of Jesus, the officer lays his hand upon him to seize him; but Mark slips out of his grasp and flees naked, leaving his robe behind him.

At that time all Christ's friends and disciples had forsaken Him. Even though a prisoner, this young man might have walked near Him and encouraged Him by his presence. But that night in his first trial, and confronted with his first great opportunity, Mark failed. He fled naked, stripped not only of his garment, but of respect and honor.

Fifteen years had passed. It was springtime at the harbor of Seleucia, the port of the great city of Antioch on the Orontes. The harbor was filled with ships—grain ships close to the wharf, taking on goods that had come down from Mesopotamia through the mountain passes to Antioch; Roman naval vessels, triremes with three banks of oars; an imperial barge of the Roman government. Everywhere confusion, animation, excitement, outcries, farewells, greetings, and a babel of tongues. Yonder was a small vessel, just getting ready to sail. The rudder was set in its groove, the anchor hoisted, the sail spread to the freshening wind, and the ship passed out through the roads into the open sea where it headed for Cyprus beyond the western horizon. On the deck of that ship were three passengers. No one paid the slightest attention to them or to their ship as it sailed out into the open sea. Yet that was the most memorable voyage in the history of mankind, for it was the beginning of the Christian odyssey. Compared with the importance of this voyage, those of Columbus, Vasco da Gama, Magellan, Hudson, and the Vikings, are nothing; for that ship carries with it a man and an idea which are to affect forever the destinies of mankind.

The three men on the deck of this vessel bound for Cyprus were Barnabas, Paul, and John Mark. Mark was a relative of the noble Barnabas, and they had taken him along as their companion or minister, that is, their helper. After journeying through Cyprus and preaching on the way, they took ship again to Perga in Pamphylia, on the southern shore of Asia Minor. There, just as they were about to depart for the high country of the interior, Mark turned back and left them. Why did he do this? Was it jealousy for his uncle Barnabas, because of the growing fame of Paul? Was it homesickness? Was it that he doubted if the heathen were worth converting? More likely it was the dangers of the rough interior country toward which Paul was heading. Even today it looks bleak and wild to the eye of the traveler who views it from the deck of a vessel in that same Gulf of Adalia. Apparently Mark's zeal had ebbed, and his courage had failed him. In the face of danger he deserted the elderly Barnabas and frail Paul, and, leaving them to scale the mountain passes by themselves, he took ship back to Syria. "John departing from them returned to Jerusalem."

John Mark had failed in his second trial. He had a great opportunity to stand by Barnabas and Paul as they went through Asia Minor to preach the Gospel on that memorable journey. Barnabas evidently did not feel so deeply about it as Paul did, for when they were ready to set out from Antioch again on the second journey, Barnabas wanted to take Mark with them; but Paul would not hear of it. "Paul thought not good to take him with them, who departed from them from Pamphylia, and went not with them to the work." Neither one would give in, and the dispute between them grew so sharp that they decided to part company. Sometimes when people cannot agree, that is the best thing to do. Barnabas took Mark and set out again for Cyprus. But Paul selected another companion, Silas, who had been highly recommended by the disciples at Antioch, and set out northward on foot, passing through Tarsus his native city on the way and then through the historic pass, the Gates of Cilicia, and so over the Taurus Mountains to Iconium, Derbe, Lystra, and the other cities and places he had visited on the first missionary journey. Mark cannot have been very happy as he sailed again for Cyprus with Barnabas and realized that he was not fit to travel with Paul. He had had a second trial and had failed. Paul had branded him as a deserter, a quitter. He was a man who had put his hand to the plow but looked backward and went backward.

Ten more years pass. Where is Mark now? Utterly discouraged by two failures? Embittered by the uncompromising attitude and the severe censure of Paul? The answer is found in a greeting or salutation at the end of Peter's first letter, written at Rome, which Peter for some reason names Babylon. "The church that is at Babylon, . . . saluteth you; and so doth Marcus my son." That tells you what happened to Mark. Mark had failed by himself, had failed dismally with Paul; but given one more chance, he had nobly "come back" and succeeded as a companion of Peter and was now worthy to have his encouragement and prayers and greetings sent along with Peter's to strengthen and cheer persecuted disciples of Christ. Peter is proud to call him "my son." There was something very touching, and very appropriate too, in that association of Peter and Mark. Both of them in their first trials had failed. None could have failed more dismally or sadly than Peter, who, on that same night in which Mark failed when he fled naked, had denied with oaths that he had ever known Jesus; but Christ in His mercy and kindness gave Peter, when he had repented, his second chance, gave him a second trial, told him to go out and feed his sheep; and Peter had grandly succeeded. No wonder, then, that he took a particular interest in John Mark.

But what of Paul? Now for him has come the sunset at Rome. Clouds and darkness are round about him, yet there are golden rays of light. Paul is in the dungeon, that cold, damp, circular dungeon, just back of the Capitoline Hill and just alongside of the Roman Forum. There, by some unknown hand, perhaps that of Luke, Paul writes his last letter. He does not expect deliverance again. He is now ready to be offered up, and the time of his departure, he says, is at hand. He has fought a good fight, kept the faith, finished the course. Now he waits for his crown. But before the end comes he wants to spend his time well. Writing to Timothy at Ephesus, he tells him to "come before winter," to bring with him the books, the writing material, the old cloak that he left behind him in the house of Carpus at Troas. Luke, he says, is with him; but Demas has gone back into the world. "Demas hath forsaken me, having loved the present world." Crescens has gone to Galatia, Titus to Dalmatia; Tychichus he has sent to Ephesus. Only Luke now is with him. So he writes to Timothy and tells him to come, and "come before winter." There is one, too, that he wants Timothy to bring with him, to be one of the chosen three who will watch with Paul in his last hours. Jesus wanted Peter and James and John, those three, to watch with him in his last trial. Paul wants these three, Timothy, Luke, and this other man, to watch with him in his final trial. And who is this third man? Is it Onesimus, Epaphroditus, Aquila, Tertius, Titus, or any other of that wonderful group of Paul's faithful friends? No! Here he is! This is the man! "Take Mark, and bring him with thee; for he is profitable to me for the ministry!"

Now, in that last great hour, with death's shadow coming down upon him, facing the "mouth of the lion," Paul wants Mark—Mark, who fled naked when he ought to have stood by Jesus, stripped not only of his clothing, but of his self-respect; Mark, who left Jesus in the hands of His enemies; Mark, who left his companions to climb alone the rugged mountains, to ford the swollen streams and face the mobs of Antioch and Lystra, and Iconium; Mark, who went back; Mark, the quitter and the coward; Mark, who separated Paul from Barnabas, the man to whom in all the world he owed the most. "Bring him with thee," Paul writes to Timothy, "for he is profitable to me for the ministry."

So Mark passes from the New Testament records. He had failed in two trials and examinations; but now he passed magna cum laude. It takes more than one defeat to make a failure. Mark had failed twice, but by repentance and perseverance and by the friendship and patience of Barnabas and Peter he was given still another chance, and this time he made good. Mark is the man who "came back." He lived to reestablish himself in the good graces of Paul and was one of the three men whom Paul wanted with him at the end. He lived to write the most graphic of the four biographies of Jesus. His symbol today is the lion.

That is the history of the man who failed and then made good. Such a history is always a stirring one and an encouraging one. When Washington took command of the army at Cambridge, he wrote to a friend that the most distressing and painful experience he had was the necessity of court-martialing an officer who had shown cowardice in the face of the enemy. But that was not the last chapter in the history of that officer. He reenlisted as a private and by his courage and fidelity and steadfastness in the midst of battle was restored again to his rank.

In 1854 a young captain in the regular army, stationed at Fort Vancouver in Oregon Territory, had fallen into bad habits. He was lonely and homesick for his young wife and baby in Missouri. Acting as quartermaster of the post, he was intoxicated on the day he was to pay the men. His superior officer, a martinet, told him he would give him a choice. He must either resign his commission or go before a court-martial. The young captain resigned his commission, took a ship down the Pacific Coast and up the Atlantic and landed penniless in New York. He would have slept on the streets, had it not been for an old army friend of Mexico days who guaranteed his bill at a hotel. Eleven years passed. On a February day in 1864, an army officer just in from the west, very ordinary in appearance, and holding a small boy by his hand, stepped up to the desk at the Willard Hotel in Washington. Indifferently the clerk handed him a pen with which to sign the register. Then, when he whirled the register around, a look of astonishment came over his face, for the words that he read were these: "U. S. Grant and son"! Ten years before dismissed from the army for intoxication; now a lieutenant general, the second since Washington, and supreme commander of the armies of the Union!

Years ago, reading the autobiography of Andrew D. White, ambassador to Germany and president of Cornell University, I came upon a passage where he related his experience as a teacher of history at the University of Michigan. There was one tall, black-haired student who was constantly stirring up trouble in his class. Dr. White had an interview with him and told him that unless he mended his ways the university would have to choose between him and its professor of history. The young man then changed his ways. But soon after in a night carousal one of the students was killed. Eight who had participated in this revel were expelled from the university, among them this young man. But before he left he came to Dr. White and said, "I want to thank you for what you have done for me, and I want you to know that I'll make a man out of myself yet." Dr. White adds that he enlisted in a regiment of Michigan cavalry and died in battle just after he had been made a brigadier general.

At this same time I had been reading in a history of the Battle of Gettysburg that on the third day of that great struggle a young brigadier general was ordered by his superior, General Kilpatrick, to charge through rocks and through timber against a brigade of infantry. The young general questioned for a moment if his superior really wanted him to make such an impossible charge. In the heat of the battle General Kilpatrick answered, "Yes. If you are afraid to lead this charge, I will lead it!" Rising in his stirrups, the young officer demanded that his superior withdraw what he had said. When he had done so and made due apology, the young brigadier drew his sword and riding to the front of his cavalry brigade led it in a magnificent, but hopeless, charge against the enemy and fell dead within their lines. I wondered if it might be that same young man about whom Dr. White had written, but whose name he had not given. I wrote him and asked, "Was that young man General Farnsworth?" And so it was! He had made good the promise that he would make a man out of himself yet.

All of us will be conscious from time to time, if not of complete breakdowns, at least of blunders, failures, and self disappointments. Which one of us has altogether and at all times done his best? But if so, there is still time for another battle. No man fails until he pronounces and accepts his own failure. The Greek theology held that no man could ever escape from his deeds, but the Christian theology says that by the power of Christ you can. Christ not only forgets and forgives, but He gives us a new name as well as a new chance. "To him that overcometh will I give . . . a white stone, and in the stone a new name written, which no man knoweth saving he that receiveth it."

13

THE TRIAL OF JUDAS

And Judas Iscariot, who also betrayed him (Matt. 10:4).

On the battlefield of Saratoga there stands a towering obelisk, commemorative of that decisive struggle of the Revolution. About its base are four deep niches, and in these are bronze figures of the generals who commanded there. In the first stands Horatio Gates, in the second, Schuyler, and in the third, Morgan. But the fourth, alas, stands empty. The soldier who won that niche of fame by his courage and valor in that battle, and in other battles of the Revolution, forfeited his right to be remembered. But below this empty niche, cut in the stone, you can read the name, Benedict Arnold. Benedict Arnold fell from the fairest heights of glory—Quebec and Saratoga—to the deepest gulfs of infamy and shame, and the empty niche in that monument shall ever stand for fallen manhood, for power prostituted, for genius soiled, for faithlessness to a sacred trust.

In heaven there is a great monument. It is a monument to the twelve apostles of the Lamb, to those who founded on earth the church of the living God. That monument is the wall of "the holy city, new Jerusalem," with its "twelve foundations." In the foundation stones are the names of the twelve apostles of the Lamb. There we shall read them: Peter, Andrew, James, John, Matthew, Philip, Thomas, Bartholomew, James the son of Alpheus, Thaddeus, and Simon the Canaanite.

But there is one name missing, and that is the name of Judas Iscariot who betrayed Him.

In Charles Kingsley's *Hypatia*, Philammon went to the witch Miriam to get a charm with which he could bring Hypatia to do his will. The witch drew from her bosom a broken talisman, and as she gazed upon it "her grim, withered features grew softer, purer, grander; and rose ennobled, for a moment, to their long-lost might-have-been, to that personal ideal which every soul brings with it into the world, which shines, dim and potential, in the face of every sleeping babe, before it has been scarred, and distorted, and encrusted in the long tragedy of life." When we see Judas fling the thirty pieces of silver down before the priests and the scribes and the Pharisees and then go out into the night and hang himself, that phrase of Kingsley's comes to mind, the "long-lost might-have-been."

Judas Iscariot is the greatest failure in history, because along with the eleven other apostles he had the highest trial of history. He was called to be an apostle, to be one of the founders of the church of Jesus Christ upon this earth. Presented with that highest opportunity, put to trial in that most august responsibility, Judas failed; hence, he is the greatest failure in history.

There is much about Judas which perplexes us and mystifies us. There is, first of all, the fact of his predestination. The Gospels record that Jesus "knew from the beginning" who it was that should betray Him. Jesus said, "Have not I chosen you twelve, and one of you is a devil?" And again, in His sublime prayer on the last night, "Those that thou gavest me I have kept, and none of them is lost, but the son of perdition; that the scripture might be fulfilled." This belongs to those things which are hid, and not to those things which have been revealed to us. All that we can do is to take Judas on the side of his own free will and his own responsibility and deal with him as a man of like passions with ourselves.

The enormity of the sin of Judas appalls one. At first it seems well-nigh incredible that a man could be for three years in the fellowship of Jesus, listen daily to His instruction and His prayers, see Him work His miracles, go out with the other apostles to preach and to heal in His name, let Him wash his feet at the Last Supper, and then go out and sell Him for thirty pieces of silver—the price of a slave. As Charles Lamb put it: "I would fain see the face of him who having dipped his hand into the same dish with the Son of man, could afterward betray him. I have no conception of such a thing; nor have I ever seen any picture, not even Leonardo's very fine one, that gave me the least idea of it." When we look at Judas Iscariot we tremble at the depths which are in Satan and at the mystery of iniquity.

If the enormity of the sin of Judas mystifies us, so also does the intensity of his remorse. At first we find it difficult to reconcile the two. If Judas was so base a man as to sell his Lord, it would seem that he was too wicked a man to suffer the remorse which is recorded of him; and, on the other hand, if he so repented, and suffered such remorse, it would seem that he could never have been so base as to have betrayed his Lord. Many of those who deal with Judas go to one of two extremes. They either dismiss him with the verdict of John—Satan entered into him—and regard him as a demon, or, at the other extreme, make him out a martyr or a hero, or at the worst, a badly mistaken man. Those who attempt to explain away or palliate the crime of Judas, proceed always from the fact of his repentance and remorse. That terrible remorse, they argue, must mean that Judas never really expected to see Christ put to trial and crucified, and, therefore, he must have been something other than a traitor.

One supposition has been that Judas, in common with the other disciples, was looking forward to the establishment by Christ of a messianic kingdom, in the temporal glories of which he would share. Judas was disappointed that Jesus did not exercise His authority as the Messiah and set up His kingdom. As the months went by and the opposition of His enemies became stronger, Judas resolved to precipitate a crisis by bringing Jesus face to face with His enemies in such a way as to compel Him to declare His messiahship and set up His throne. In order to accomplish this, and at a time when the crowds were in Jerusalem attending the Passover, Judas decided to play the part of seeming desertion and treason. But when he had played that part, and to his amazement and horror Jesus permitted Himself to be taken by His enemies and condemned to death, overcome with remorse and despair at his mistake, Judas brought the money back to the priests, and, flinging it down before them, exclaimed, "I have sinned, in that I have betrayed the innocent blood," and then went out and hanged himself. Here, at the worst, Judas was an ambitious man, seeking worldly power and gain through his association with Jesus, but never at heart or with intent a traitor.

Of a somewhat similar nature is the sketch of Judas Iscariot in a famous essay by Thomas De Quincey, a defense of Judas in which the beauty of the literary style of the author is matched only by the complete improbability of his hypothesis. According to De Quincey, Judas understood from the Scripture that Christ must be betrayed into the hands of His enemies before He could assert His royal power and take His throne. He therefore volunteered to play the part of the traitor, not for worldly gain, but with the sincere desire to forward the cause of Christ. But when he realized his colossal mistake—that he had played the traitor in vain and that Christ was delivered up to be crucified—tortured with remorse, he went out and hanged himself. "He fell into fierce despair; his heart broke, and under that storm of affliction he hanged himself."

Interesting as that sketch of Judas is, it must be dismissed as only the dream of an opium eater, for however noble or tragic such a Judas might have been, he is not the Judas we meet in the pages of the Gospel and of whom his Master solemnly said, "It had been good for that man if he had not been born." No, Judas was not a demon, neither was he a martyr who made a tragic mistake in his plans for his Master. Judas was a man of like passions with us. The disciples all recognized that, for when Jesus made the announcement of His betrayal, no one asked, "Is it Judas?" but each one asked, "Lord, is it I?"

In contrast with the other apostles, Judas failed in his highest trial. They were men like Judas, but their association with Jesus brought out the best that was in them. All of them, too, had unlovely traits, some of which are recorded. Peter, with all his splendid characteristics, had a natural inclination to boastfulness and to cowardice. Thomas was gloomy and melancholy and inclined to doubt. James and John were violent and intolerant.

All the disciples were, in a way, selfish and disputed one with another as to places of honor in the kingdom of Christ. But in the school of Jesus these traits were checked and restrained. At the end of His association with them Jesus could say that He had kept them by the power of God and that "none of them is lost," not one of them had failed in his trial, except Judas, "the son of perdition."

The same summer sun which ripens the grain also ripens the weeds. In his association with Jesus Judas grew worse rather than better. One morning in the obscure Judean village of Kerioth a Hebrew mother clasped her baby to her breast with all the love and hope with which mothers clasp a newborn child. The mother looked down into the face of her babe and wondered what manner of person this child would be. When he had come to manhood Jesus passed through his village, and he heard Jesus speak. Perhaps he saw Him work miracles. He listened to His words on the way of life and the kingdom of God. The heart of Judas must have thrilled at the person and teaching of Jesus. When Jesus said to him one day, "Follow me," and then on another occasion, after a whole night spent in prayer, formally chose him as one of the twelve apostles, it must have been because of the native capacity, the potential good that there was in Judas. We cannot think of Jesus calling Judas into the band of the apostles just as one would choose an actor to take the part of a villain in a play. In his first association with Jesus, no doubt the natural avarice and other unlovely traits in Judas were checked. But, in contrast with the other apostles, that was not a final influence. They became better in their association with Jesus. Judas became worse. The light in the soul of Judas, which had flared up anew in his first contact with Christ, had become darkness, until at length he went out into the night, a traitor and a murderer. And how great was that darkness!

What were the motives which actuated Judas? Undoubtedly, one of them was avarice—perhaps it was the chief one. Judas had a capacity for finance. He liked to deal with money, and for that reason, I suppose, was appointed the treasurer of the apostolic band. Judas "had the bag." None of them knew it at the time, probably not John himself, but John says of him afterward that in this capacity as the keeper of the bag, the treasurer of their company, "he was a thief." Jesus could feed the multitude with a few loaves and fishes and the cattle upon a thousand hills were His, and yet for His own needs and those of His disciples He depended upon that bag, that common treasury, for His daily bread. It lets us know, then, how low Judas had fallen when we are told that he pilfered from that treasury! Probably it was when he was well along in apostasy and treason that he began to steal.

The other Gospels all relate the criticism of Mary's beautiful gift when she anointed the feet of Jesus with the "ointment of spikenard, very costly," and wiped them with her hair. But it is John who tells us that it was Judas who said, "Why was not this ointment sold for three hundred pence, and given to the poor?" According to John, Judas was thinking only of himself, and how if those three hundred pence had been given into the treasury, supposedly for the poor, he would have had that much more to steal. There, too, is another index to the state of mind to which Judas had come; not only would he steal from the common treasury, but he would even steal money that had been given for the sake of the poor. This prepares us for the climax of his avarice, when for thirty pieces of silver he betrayed Jesus into the hands of His enemies.

Some have tried to make out that whatever motive led Judas, it must have been something other than avarice, for thirty pieces of silver was too paltry a sum to move a man to such a colossal crime. But surely they who say this forget what Jesus said on the subject of money, what the Bible repeatedly says about the love of money and the peril of riches, and, alas, what man's history has to say on that subject. Once a man came to see me and to demand of me, like that man who once came to Christ in the Gospels, that I command his sister to divide the inheritance with him and make what, he claimed, was just restitution. In declining to act I cited what Jesus said on that occasion, "Who made me a judge or a divider over you?" Then the angry man said, "If there is a hell, she is in it!" No; thirty pieces was not too small a bait for Judas! Thirty pieces of silver has not been too small a sum to corrupt the soul of man, to show men the way down to hell, and to make them wish to take others to hell with them. Judas, therefore, preaches the greatest sermon in the Bible on that text of Jesus, "Take heed, and beware of covetousness: for a man's life consisteth not in the abundance of the things which he possesseth."

Another possible, and even probable, motive with Judas was his disappointment that Christ did not set up an earthly kingdom. The first definite information that we have that Judas was on the road to ruin was not long after Jesus had refused to let the people, enthusiastic over His miracles, make Him a king. After this Jesus had made it clear to His disciples that His path would be the way of rejection and sorrow and death. Many of His disciples, that is, the disciples at large, about this time "went back and walked no more with him." Seeing them leave Him, Jesus turned sadly to the twelve, and said, "Will ye also go away?" Peter then gave his great answer, "Lord, to whom shall we go? thou hast the words of eternal life." But the only reply of Jesus was, "Have I not chosen you twelve, and one of you is a devil?" The whole association of these events indicates that it was about this time that Judas began to decline from Christ.

When Jesus said, "One of you is a devil," we must not take it as meaning that Judas was a demon, for about the same time, when Jesus had announced to the disciples His approaching humiliation and crucifixion, and Peter remonstrated with Him, saying, "Be it far from thee, Lord: this shall not be unto thee," Jesus, who a moment before had so highly commended Peter for his great confession, now said to him, "Get thee behind me, Satan; thou art an offense unto me; for thou savorest not the things that be of God, but those that be of men." Jesus did not mean there that Peter was Satan, a devil, any more than he meant that Judas was a devil, but that both of them were taking an attitude which would please Satan rather than God. Whenever anyone of us yields to that which is evil, in thought, word, or deed, to that degree Satan enters into us. We can think, then, of the increasing disappointment of Judas as he saw his worldly expectations vanish, until at length he resolved to desert Jesus and to get what financial gain he could out of it.

Jealousy also was a likely motive in the heart of Judas. Race and group feeling was intense at that time. Judas seems to be the only one of the apostles who was not a Galilean, for he came from the village of Kerioth in Judd. It is altogether likely that the other disciples looked upon Judas as sort of a stranger and interloper in their midst. Judas may have resented, too, the prominence of Peter and James and John, who formed an inner circle within the apostolic band.

There is indication, also, that in the final dark act of Judas—selling Jesus for thirty pieces of silver and betraying Him with a kiss—he was moved by vindictive resentment toward Jesus. His early enthusiasm by this time had turned to scorn. A year before, when Jesus said, "One of you is a devil," Judas must have known that Jesus knew all that was in his heart. He no doubt resented the rebuke that Jesus had given him when he objected to Mary's beautiful and costly gift, when Jesus had told him to "let her alone," that what she had done would "be spoken of for a memorial of her" wherever His Gospel should be preached in the ages to come. That, no doubt, rankled in the heart of Judas. The more he saw the gulf that was between him and the pure life of Christ, instead of repenting, the more he hardened his own heart. The fact that he betrayed Jesus with a kiss certainly points to a vindictive malignancy and a satisfaction of revenge. There were other ways by which he could have pointed out the victim, but that was the way in which he chose to do it; and sweet, indeed, must have been that treacherous kiss to his now hating and vindictive spirit.

No man goes to his doom without warning and appeals. Certainly Judas did not. When you review his history and then read through the Gospels again, there seem to be so many occasions when what Jesus says has a solemn and particular application to the traitor: what He said about covetousness; and His great question, "What shall it profit a man, if he shall gain the whole world, and lose his own soul?" And those solemn, searching words warning His hearers against permitting the light which was in them to become darkness. When you read through those passages, you must always think of Judas.

There were special appeals, too, as when Jesus said, after Judas had criticized Mary's gift, "Me ye have not always." But the most extraordinary, and to us the most diabolical, thing in the treason of Judas is that even after he had covenanted with the scribes and Pharisees to deliver up Jesus to them Judas went back and took his place at the Last Supper. When Jesus girded Himself with a towel and went round the table, washing the feet of the disciples, what did Judas think when he felt the pressure of the Master's hand upon his foot? I like to think of that touch of Christ as a last appeal to Judas. Some say that when Jesus gave him the whispered command, "That thou doest, do quickly," He meant that now that Judas was completely given over to his infamy, he must proceed at once to carry it out. But I like to think that when He said, "That thou doest, do quickly," He was giving Judas one more chance to return and repent. Again, at their final meeting—and how moving that final meeting between Judas and Jesus was—at that final meeting in the garden of Gethsemane, after Judas had bestowed his traitorous kiss, Jesus said to him, "Friend, wherefore art thou come?" Still He called him "friend," as if reluctant to give him over to the ranks of His enemies. I wonder if that was not a last appeal to Judas? But if so, that and all other appeals were in vain.

Then came the terrible awakening and the remorse of Judas, when he flung the blood money down before the priests and said, "I have sinned, in that I have betrayed the innocent blood," and then went out and hanged himself. Much has been written and spoken about the difference between the repentance of Judas and the repentance of Peter. I would not attempt to state that difference. So far as each felt a terrible and overwhelming sense of the cruel wrong he had done the Master, I cannot see that there was much difference. But this difference, at least, is clear (clear, and how solemn it is, too): the repentance of Judas, whatever it was, came too late. He had sinned away his day of grace and had gone to his own place.

The remorse and the end of Judas preach a great sermon on conscience, and the power of conscience to punish and torment. Here we see hell with all its terrors this side of the grave. Here is "where their worm dieth not, and the fire is not quenched." The deathless sting, the quenchless flame of an avenging conscience!

The last we hear of Judas is after the Resurrection and the Ascension. Peter assembled the disciples and called upon them to elect a successor to Judas. When they prayed together for divine guidance as between two men, Justus and Matthias, they said: "Thou, Lord, which knowest the hearts of all men, shew whether of these two thou hast chosen, that he may take part of this ministry and apostleship, from which Judas by transgression fell, that he might go to his own place." I feel sure that it was Peter who offered that prayer. How wise and noble his restraint is. No execration of Judas, no expression of horror at his crime, but that calm, judicial, and forever solemn statement that he had gone "to his own place." That was not the place that Christ had in mind for him when He called him to the apostleship. Judas might have stood today as one of that illustrious band, the "Glorious Company of the Apostles." He might have had his name written along with the other twelve apostles of the Lamb upon the foundation stones of the wall of the city of God, the new Jerusalem. But instead of that, Judas went to his own place—the place of his own making, the place of his own choosing, the place against which he was repeatedly warned. Judas went to his own place. There is the secret of divine retribution.

> The tissue of the Life to be
> We weave with colors all our own,
> And in the field of Destiny
> We reap as we have sown.

Judas is not a sermon to preach to outsiders, to strangers to Christ, to His open and avowed enemies. Judas is the sermon to preach to the inside circle, to the disciples, to the friends of Christ. In his great trial as a friend of Christ, as one of the twelve apostles, Judas failed. He vanished into darkness. He went "to his own place." Every member of a Christian church, everyone who has sat down at the Lord's Table, and everyone who has confessed himself as a follower of Christ is on trial as to that relationship. It is the highest and most momentous trial of life. How is your trial proceeding? What effect is your association with Christ, through His church, having upon your life? The church is the body of Christ. How faithful have you been to it? Oh, when we think of that, when we reflect that each one of us is on trial with regard to Jesus Christ as Judas was, then what can we say for ourselves but what the other disciples said that night when Jesus announced that one of them should betray Him: "Lord, is it I?"

14

THE TRIAL OF PAUL

There was given to me a thorn in the flesh (2 Cor. 12:7).

When a Roman emperor had a triumph, it was the custom for a slave to ride with him in his chariot, and ever and anon, amid the plaudits of the multitude and the clouds of incense, remind his master that he, too, was but a man. Paul, a man of many visions and extraordinary experiences, as well as immense native talent and genius, had a thorn in the flesh which daily reminded him that he was a man of like passions with those to whom he preached.

There were so many things of which Paul might have boasted—his intellect, his talent, his learning, his courage, his endurance, his achievements. But the only thing of which he dares to boast is his infirmity. Enemies at Corinth had sown the seeds of suspicion and distrust in the minds of the converts and Christians of that city. His right to be an apostle had been questioned, and it had been broadly hinted that he was either a fraud or a fool. It is in connection with these charges that Paul comes to speak of his visions. Yet he does it with reluctance, saying, "There is nothing to be gained by this sort of thing, but . . . I am obliged to boast" (2 Cor. 12:1 *Moffatt*). What he means is that he mentions these unusual experiences only because he is compelled to do so by the false charges of his enemies. Thus he comes to his visions and revelations. There were many that he might have mentioned, and with the circumstances of which we are familiar. But the one which he mentions is an experience of which we know nothing save this reference to it. It occurred fourteen years before the writing of this letter, which would seem to locate it about the time of the beginning of his work as a missionary at Antioch.

The experience is so wonderful that he cannot tell whether his whole body shared in it or not; and as for what he saw and heard, that was a secret which he could not repeat. Caught up into the heavens, he had seen and heard things of which he might reasonably boast; and yet, upon second thought, he says, lest his doing so should lead men to think that he was something greater than he really was, a sort of superman, he will not boast even of this wonderful trance, but will boast only in the weakness which followed it. Lest he should become proud, because of this and other visions and unusual experiences through which he has passed, he was given "a thorn in the flesh." He describes it as "the messenger of Satan," to smite him and beat him as with the fist. Yet, although Satan was the agent, the permission, as in the case of Job, came from God. The thorn in the flesh was given him of God, and the purpose was to keep him from undue pride.

WHAT WAS THE THORN?

So frank as to the fact of the thorn and the purpose of it, Paul preserves a noble reticence as to what it was. The main thing with him was the purpose of it and the effect which it produced upon his spiritual life. The theories as to the nature of Paul's thorn divide themselves into two classes—figurative and literal. Among the figurative explanations is the idea that by a thorn in the flesh Paul means the persecution or slanders of a personal foe. Even today, it is not unusual to speak of unkind or hostile persons as a thorn in one's side; and such a thorn, indeed, can be very sore, annoying, and humbling, to a degree that the man who suffers from that sort of thorn will sometimes be tempted to forget his friends and think only of his foes. There is no question as to the number and malignancy of Paul's enemies. No one could have put on his grave that sad and ignoble epitaph, "He never had an enemy." The

foes of Paul trailed him over the world, traducing his character, aspersing his honesty, questioning his apostleship, and in
every way trying to blacken his reputation and undermine his
influence. One of these enemies, Alexander the coppersmith,
he mentions by name, saying that he "did me much evil," and
warns Timothy to be on the lookout against him. It is worth
noting, too, that in speaking of some of these enemies who
persecuted him, Paul refers to them as Satan disguised as an
angel of light; and here he speaks of his thorn as a "messenger
of Satan." But such an enemy was nothing new or unusual in
Paul's history.

Another figurative explanation of the thorn in the flesh is
that it was a temptation in the body. This is perhaps due in
part to the translation in the Vulgate Bible, *stimulus carnis*, "an
incitement of the flesh." At first hearing, it shocks one to think
of the great apostle as subject to any such temptation as this.
Yet we must remember that Paul was a man and not an angel,
and that he goes out of the way to tell men that he does not
want them to think of him as higher and holier than he is.

In this connection it is well to recall Paul's reference to the
fierce civil war that raged within him between the law of sin
and his spiritual aspirations: how he was bound, as it were, to a
body of death and, resolving to do the good and resist the evil,
often failed to do the good that he would and did the evil that
he would not. We think, too, of those earnest and solemn
words, how he kept his body under, severely and constantly
disciplining it, lest after having preached to others he himself
should make shipwreck of his ministry. Certainly such inflic-
tion of temptation would be humbling in the extreme to a man
of the high visions and mighty aspirations of Paul; and if this
really were his thorn in the flesh, it would bring him down
into the ranks of the ordinary man, to be our comrade in the
grim battle of life, who must draw his sword and fight against
even bodily temptations like any ordinary person. It pours a
wealth of meaning, too, into those great passages which ring
with the note of overcoming and triumph, telling to himself
and to the world and to the ages how he is made to triumph in
Christ and to come off conqueror and more than conqueror.

But we pass now from the figurative to the literal explanation.

On the face of it, that it was some literal, physical affliction seems the most natural interpretation; and for a man of great visions, great gifts, and great ambitions, a constant, disabling, and perhaps disgusting, disease would be very humbling. There is a democracy in sickness and pain, as there is in death. In the hospital I see some lying on the beds side by side in the wards, and others in well-appointed private rooms with flowers and special nurses; but sickness and pain are great levelers, and there is no difference between pain in the ward and pain in the private apartment.

Among the possible physical ailments answering to a thorn in the flesh there has been suggested an unhealed wound left by the scourgings or stonings through which Paul passed. He says he was thrice "beaten with rods," the fearful Roman castigation to which Christ was subjected and which not infrequently produced death. And five times he received thirty-nine stripes from the Jews, and once, at Lystra, he was stoned. If some of those wounds never healed and left a running sore, it would indeed have been a thorn in the flesh, weakening, disabling, and rendering him offensive to men's sensibilities, as is hinted at in the letter to the Galatians.

Another suggestion has been epilepsy. This would be intermittent, answering to the description that something "buffeted" him, and was associated with the influence of Satan. It is also revolting to him who beholds such a seizure. If he suffered from such a complaint, this would explain why Paul almost never traveled alone and for a great part of the time had a physician, Luke, with him.

Another explanation is malarial fever. Paul says in the letter to the Galatians that it was "through infirmity of the flesh" that he had preached the Gospel to them. This would seem to mean that he came to *their* cities and preached to *them*, instead of going elsewhere, because of a physical ailment. It will be remembered that Paul and his three companions, leaving Cyprus, crossed to the Asiatic mainland at Perga. But instead of remaining there, they ascended to the high tablelands of Asia Minor and preached at Antioch and Lystra and Derbe and Iconium. The country about Perga was malarial, and the inhabitants were wont to make annual migrations to the highlands.

If Paul's letter is addressed to the churches of Galatia visited on this missionary journey, then an attack of fever would explain his not tarrying at Perga and his saying that "through infirmity of the flesh" he happened to preach the Gospel to the Galatians. It would explain, too, his strong aversion for John Mark who turned back at Perga, if indeed he deserted Paul under these circumstances.

Another and, it seems to me, the most plausible explanation is some kind of a disease of the eyes, fearfully prevalent in the East, then and now. Ophthalmia in certain forms is very painful and can be likened to the piercings of a stake or a thorn, and in its worst forms is disgusting to those who look upon one so afflicted. The ancients had a custom of spitting in the presence of one so afflicted in order to render themselves immune from such an attack. In referring to his past relationship with the Galatians and their former loyalty, Paul reminds them how they did not despise or reject the temptation of his flesh. The literal meaning of the word translated as "reject" is "to spit out." Referring to their loyalty, immediately after this, Paul says that they were so devoted to him that "if it had been possible, ye would have plucked out your own eyes, and have given them to me." This sentence becomes luminous if Paul's thorn in the flesh was a disease of the eyes. We know, too, that Paul generally employed an amanuensis, taking pains merely to put his own signature to a letter to guard against forgery. One explanation might be that his mind worked so rapidly that his hand, in a vain effort to keep up with the mind, left an illegible record. But a not unreasonable explanation is that Paul suffered from poor vision. The letter to the Galatians is an ardent appeal to them to return to their former faith and loyalty, and at least the concluding section of the letter was written by Paul in his own hand. He says, "Ye see how large a letter [or, literally, what big letters] I have written unto you with mine own hand." There is the suggestion there that Paul wrote at least a part of the epistle with his own hand in order that these characters, painfully traced because of his failing eyesight, would touch their hearts and move them to return to their former loyalty.

Dr. John Brown, the delightful author of the great dog story

Rab and His Friends, supports this idea that Paul's thorn in the flesh was a disease of the eye by calling to mind an incident at his trial before the Sanhedrin. At the opening of the trial, Paul made an asseveration of his integrity and godly life, whereupon the high priest, Ananias, commanded the guards to smite him upon the mouth. At this Paul burst out, "God shall smite thee, thou whited wall: for sittest thou to judge me after the law, and commandest me to be smitten contrary to the law?" One of the bystanders said, "Revilest thou God's high priest?" And Paul responded, "I wist not, brethren, that he was the high priest: for it is written, 'Thou shalt not speak evil of the ruler of thy people.'" One interpretation is that Paul was speaking satirically, and that Ananias was no real and just high priest. The other is that Paul spoke impulsively, and when he said, "I wist not," he meant that in the affront offered him, he did not stop to consider who had inflicted it. But a third explanation is that Paul did not see the high priest and did not know that the order had come from him.

The question of the nature of the thorn has always been and always will be an interesting and not unprofitable theme, for it brings us to a consideration of the great hardships which the apostle endured. But Paul himself was silent on the subject. Perhaps he will tell us when we see him; perhaps not. What he is clear about and what we do know is the purpose of the thorn.

THE PURPOSE OF THE THORN

The purpose of the thorn was to keep Paul from spiritual pride, the sin that made angels fall and seems to have been the fountain source of all other sins. Paul might have been tempted to think of himself more highly than he ought to think, or to have others think so of him. He might have forgotten, when he preached redemption, that he himself was a sinner. But this thorn in the flesh kept the fact of his humanity and his own need ever before him. Thus, he who exalts Christ as Redeemer is the one who ever sees himself as the chief of sinners. That was the purpose of Paul's thorn—to keep him from spiritual pride. The purpose of the thorn in our lives may not be just the same as that. Nevertheless, the thorn is pushed in always for some good purpose.

How many different kinds of thorns there are! Thorns in the mind, and thorns in the flesh. The throng with whom you mingle on the street or with whom you sit in the church—all of them at some time or other have a thorn in the flesh. Whether it is covered by rags or concealed by fine garments, the thorn is there, piercing, throbbing, aching. With one it may be physical, a disease which handicaps in the race of life, a weakness which disqualifies for service, or an affliction in the way of physical suffering which has a history of transgression. With another it may be the frustration of ambition, the disappointment of hope, the throbbing of conscience or remorse, the friction of domestic unhappiness, or the slanderous malignancy of an enemy. If everyone were to pluck his thorn and display it to the world, what a collection it would be! If I were to invite everyone in the church to march down the aisles and deposit his particular thorn on the pavement in front of the pulpit, what a heap of strange thorns in the flesh, in the mind, in the heart, it would be!

Diverse as the thorns may be, every thorn serves some purpose. It is not an accident, but like Paul's, is given of God, although the agency may seem to us nothing less than satanic. What are some of the possible purposes of the thorn? As in the case of Paul, it may be to keep us humble. At the time of a serious illness, Grover Cleveland in a letter wrote these words: "I have learned how weak the strongest man is under God's decrees and I see in a new light the necessity of doing my allotted work in the full apprehension of the coming night." "Oh! why should the spirit of mortal be proud?"

A second purpose of a thorn is to warn us and keep us from sin. Pain turns our thought inward, and therefore has a disciplinary and purifying effect. If one thorn today is more intense in its pain than a former one, it probably is because we did not take heed to a less severe warning. It is easy enough to connect the thorn in the lives of other people with their faults and short-comings, to say that this or that was a judgment, or that it was the very thing to take him down and warn him, the very thing he needed.

A third purpose of the thorn is to make us more useful. Why did Paul pray so earnestly that that thorn might be plucked from his flesh? Not merely that he might be relieved from the distress and the pain and the humiliation of it, but that he might have greater freedom and success in his work for Christ, for he supposed that the thorn was hampering him and hindering him. But when Christ tells him that He will not pluck the thorn but will give him grace to bear it, out of his weakness make him strong, and thus make him a greater servant of Christ—when Paul understands that, he says that he can even rejoice now in his thorn and glory in his infirmity, "for when I am weak, then am I strong." Suppose Paul's prayer had been answered at once and that thorn had been plucked? Then no such sermon as this would ever have been preached, and thousands upon thousands of Christian souls would never have been inspired and comforted, as they have been inspired and comforted, with the story of Paul and his thorn in the flesh. But it is not so easy to connect our own thorns with what is lacking or what is wrong in our lives.

THE PRAYER AND THE ANSWER

Paul, like Christ, had his Gethsemane, and in his agony, like Christ, he prayed for relief from his burden. But the prayer was not answered; not, that is, in the form which Paul had desired, for the thorn was not plucked. What Paul tells us of his thorn and the prayer he made at that time is one of the most illuminating of all scriptural teachings on the subject of unanswered prayer. Paul certainly had as much earnestness and as much faith as any Christian of whom we have heard. Yet his earnest prayer that the thorn be plucked was not answered. If God did that, if He just granted us anything and everything that we asked in the name of Christ, then the name of Christ in our prayers would be like the fabled ring which a despot gave to one of his subjects, the presentation of which would grant him any favor that he asked. Always in our prayers there must be the condition and reservation of Christ's prayer, "Nevertheless, not as I will, but as thou wilt." No one ought to pray unless he is perfectly willing that God should refuse to answer his prayer, if by refusal, the greater good would result to him. Thus when he is weak, he is strong.

There is a sense in which we can say that every earnest prayer is answered by God. Moses on Nebo's lonely mountain prayed that he might cross over the Jordan with the children of Israel into the land of Canaan. But God said No—"I have caused thee to see it with thine eyes, but thou shalt not go over." But now, centuries afterward, there is Moses, standing in glory with Elijah on the Mount of Transfiguration in the land of Canaan and talking with Christ concerning His atonement which He should accomplish at Jerusalem. David lay groaning on the ground and prayed earnestly for the life of the child that had been born to him and Bathsheba. The prayer, as to its particularity, was not answered; but David was given grace and comfort and spoke those words which through all the ages that have passed since have brought comfort and consolation to fathers and mothers mourning over a little child, "Can I bring him back again? I shall go to him, but he shall not return to me." Jesus prayed three times in the Garden of Gethsemane, "If it be possible, let this cup pass from me." The cup did not pass from Him. That was not possible, even with God, if the world was to be redeemed. But there appeared a great angel from heaven strengthening Christ, giving Him strength to say, "As thou wilt," and to drink that bitter, bitter cup for our eternal salvation.

Augustine in his *Confessions* tells us how when he was planning to leave his home in North Africa and go to Italy his mother prayed earnestly that he might be kept from sailing, for she feared that his going to Rome would mean the ruin of the soul. But by a stratagem Augustine managed to get away while his mother was spending the night in a hospice on the shore. He had told her he was going on the ship to visit a friend, but when the morning dawned the ship had sailed with him. Monica, brokenhearted and disappointed, felt that her prayer had not been answered. It had not been answered as to its detail, but as to its substance it was answered. For what was she praying? She was praying that her son might be restrained from going to Europe so that his soul might be saved. And yet it was that trip to Italy that led Augustine, step by step, to the great change which came over him that day in the garden at Milan when he heard the voice of God and found Christ as his Redeemer. So Augustine wrote, looking back over that history: "But thou in thy hidden wisdom didst grant the substance of her desire, yet refused the thing she prayed for, in order that thou mightest effect in me what she was ever praying for."

Do men gather grapes of thorns? Yes, sometimes, when it is this kind of a thorn and taken as Paul took it. Paul's thorn blossomed. God may be able to make more use of you thorned than thornless. When you are tempted to wonder why this particular thorn was thrust into you, remember, as quaint and loving Samuel Rutherford put it, that God has ten thousand thorns which He might have chosen, but this is the one which He has selected for you.

When your thorn troubles you, think of Paul! His thorn never embittered him, never turned him back from his work, never discouraged him, never made him doubt the goodness of God. Take up your own cross and follow Him who in your weakness can make you strong, that Savior who for your sake endured, not one thorn in the flesh, but a crown of thorns upon the accursed tree.

15

THE LAST TRIAL OF JESUS

Being in an agony (Luke 22:44).

Some years ago, I had occasion to change trains at a railroad junction in the southern part of Texas. It was a wretched, straggling town, the streets mere gashes through the red loam. There were several warehouses and a collection of general stores, with mules and horses tied at the rail in front. On top of a barren hill was the courthouse, and scattered about without any semblance of order, depressing in their location and appearance, were the houses of the inhabitants. There was a brick church, not more attractive than the other buildings. But as I passed by, I could make out in the large stained glass window the figure of Christ kneeling in Gethsemane. The glass was cheap and the window poorly executed; but cheap glass and poor execution could not altogether distort the majesty and pathos of Christ kneeling in His agony for the salvation of souls. The miserable hamlet seemed to take on a certain dignity and worth now, because one realized that He who was represented there as entering into His agony in Gethsemane had suffered and died for the people who lived in this town. He suffered and died for you, for me. If you had been the only person in the world, still Christ for you would have entered into Gethsemane.

A long distance from Jerusalem to Texas, from Gethsemane with its olive trees and its shadows beyond the Cedron to that brick church in the forlorn town, and almost nineteen hundred years between the incident which took place in Gethsemane and its crude reproduction in glass in the window of the church. Yet time and distance take nothing from the pathos, the grandeur, and the tragedy of Gethsemane.

We commonly speak of the three temptations of Christ, but there is no reason to think that His temptations were concluded at the end of the third temptation, when He said to the tempter, "Get thee behind me, Satan." If Christ was tempted only at the outset of His ministry and never again, then it could hardly be said that He was tempted in all points like as we are. Temptation comes back to men again and again. No one ever gets beyond the danger line of temptation. Youth, middle life, old age have their dangerous hours and dangerous places.

> The gray-haired saint may fall at last,
> The surest guide a wanderer prove;
> Death only binds us fast
> To the bright shore of love.

Luke tells us that when Satan was repulsed the third time "he departed from him for a season." That it was only for a season we may judge from what Christ said to Peter. After Peter had hailed Jesus as the Messiah and the Son of God and had been signally honored and blessed by Christ for his confession, Jesus began to show to His disciples that He must be crucified at Jerusalem. Not understanding the meaning of this, Peter undertook to hold Christ back from His passion, saying, "Lord: this shall not be unto thee." Then Christ turned upon Peter, whom but a moment ago He had so highly blessed, and said, "Get thee behind me, Satan; thou art an offense unto me; for thou savorest not the things that be of God, but those that be of men." Through Peter, and making use of his beautiful loyalty and affection for Christ, the tempter was trying to persuade Jesus, just as he did in the wilderness, to take some other path than that appointed by God for the redemption of the world. In the Garden of Gethsemane we have the grand climax to the temptation of Christ. It was the final assault of

Satan. He attacks Christ on the eve of the crucifixion and at the very foot of the cross. The curtain rises and falls upon Christ in a struggle with the great adversary of His work and the great enemy of human souls.

Gethsemane, even more than Calvary, is the most mysterious and the most terrible and yet the most triumphant moment in the life of Jesus. Even more than Calvary it exerts a strange fascination over men. The Nativity with its songs and its scenes charms us. Our hearts burn within us as we listen to Christ pronounce His beatitudes or behold Him opening the eyes of the blind, healing the leper, or giving the dead son back to His mother at the gates of the city of Nain. But calvaries and crucifixions take the deepest hold on the race. In Gethsemane the greatest thing in human experience—suffering—is witnessed in the greatest of those who came into the world, and at the moment of its greatest intensity.

The disciples marched that night to the music of a hymn. Ever since, the church of Christ has been marching to the music of her song. "When they had sung a hymn," Matthew tells us, "they went out." To John alone we are indebted for the route of their journey from the chamber where they had celebrated the Supper to Gethsemane. John tells us that they crossed "the brook Cedron," literally "the dark torrent of the cedars." The brook was dark because it was stained with the blood of the sacrifices which drained from the temple area into it. Now the great Sacrifice Himself, on His way to the altar, crosses the dark brook. And with Him are His disciples, with only "the son of perdition" missing. Christ went to a well-known place for His last vigil and thus made easy the traitor's task. Considerate love would help even the arm that was lifted to strike him. The owner of this garden is unnamed. Yet he ought not to be forgotten. Whoever he was he had given Christ the free use of this orchard and had told Him that He and His disciples could come and go whenever they pleased.

Somewhere near the gate, Christ left Matthew, Thomas, Nathanael, Philip, and the rest of the eight, and taking with Him Peter and James and John proceeded further into the garden. These three had stood with Him on the Mount of Transfiguration and had seen His glory. Now they are to descend with Him into the valley of His humiliation and behold His agony. But even these three must remain apart from Him at least a stone's cast.

There, all by Himself, Christ entered into His agony. The word "agony" is a transliteration rather than a translation, that is, it merely produces the sound of the original Greek word which means "the struggle" or "the contest." Christ entered into His struggle, His trial, His contest, His last battle with temptation.

The utter solitude of Christ here impresses us with its intensity. We can hear Him say in the words of the Twenty-second Psalm, afterward quoted by Him on the cross: "My God, my God, why hast thou forsaken me? why art thou so far from helping me? . . . Be not far from me, for trouble is near; for there is none to help. . . . Be not thou far from me, O Lord: O my strength, haste thee to help me." Or, in the words of the prophet, "I have trodden the winepress alone; and of the people there was none with me. . . . I looked, and there was none to help; and I wondered that there was none to uphold."

Matthew and Mark tell us that Jesus "began to be sorrowful and very heavy." This term "very heavy" is an unusual one. It occurs elsewhere in the New Testament only in Paul's letter to the Philippians, where he is telling them about his friend Epaphroditus who had come with a gift from the church at Philippi, how Epaphroditus was "full of heaviness" for his friends in the distant city. The word, then, strikes the note of longing and homesickness. Christ was far from His Father, far from His heavenly home. As He contemplated the price He must pay for the world's redemption, a homesickness of the soul came over Him. He "began to be sorrowful and very heavy." How sudden and complete the change in Christ from that calm confidence and self-possession and assurance which characterized Him as He sat with the disciples at the Last Supper and discoursed to them concerning His death and resurrection and the coming of His kingdom. Then all was peace and strength. Now the horror of great darkness is upon Him.

It is His last and greatest recoil from the sinner's cup. Mark in his account gives one of his graphic strokes when he tells us that Jesus "began to be sore amazed." What was He amazed at? What could amaze or surprise the Son of God? It was His wonder at the sinfulness of sin—the blackness of that abyss into which He must descend in order to rescue the souls of men. There are some things which we can contemplate at a distance, but which we realize only when they come upon us. When he was dying, the great pictorial preacher, Thomas Guthrie, said to his family that he had often in his sermons described deathbeds and dying scenes, but the reality was something far beyond anything which he had described. You can contemplate at a distance what you know must take place as the great acts in your mortal probation are fulfilled; but you will never know what they are until their hour comes. When the Greeks came to inquire for Jesus, and in their eager inquiry Jesus saw a token of the triumph of His Gospel, He rejoiced in His heart. But when He remembered what the price was to be, He cried out in distress, "Let this cup pass from me!" It was hard enough to contemplate it at a distance, but now that hour has struck, and the price He must pay, the experience through which He must pass for the salvation of men, is upon Him in all its terrible reality.

Each one of the evangelists contributes his own distinctive stroke and color to this great scene in the garden. It is Luke who tells us that as He prayed in His agony "his sweat was as it were great drops of blood falling down to the ground." This gives you the complete picture of mental anguish, the effect of which upon the body is too well-established a fact to call for comment. Perhaps the marks of that bloody sweat remained upon the face and the body and garments of Jesus. Unless Christ Himself related it to His disciples the only way they could have known it was by observing it, not when they were watching, for they were sleeping and not watching, but when Christ was through with His struggle. Perhaps too, the mob who came to arrest Him, and fell back before Him amazed, were amazed at the crimson stains upon Him. Coming out from His agony in the garden to march to the cross for the world's redemption, Christ could well have been described in the words of the prophet, "Who is this that cometh from Edom, with dyed garments from Bozrah? . . . Wherefore art thou red in thine apparel, and thy garments like him that treadeth in the winefat?" Herod need not in mockery have put his gorgeous robe upon the shoulders of Christ, for this blood-stained robe was the mark of His kingship. It had upon it the marks of Gethsemane's bloody sweat when the soldiers cast their dice over it. One of those profane legionaries won the toss and secured the robe, wore it on the march, wore it in battle. But that robe, after all, is the church's great possession. It is the red banner that tells of my crimson sin and of God's unfathomable and redeeming love.

Wherefore this agony, this bloody sweat, this thrice-reiterated prayer, "Oh, my Father, if it be possible, let this cup pass from me"? Whatever difficulty we have in telling what that agony *was*, we have little difficulty in saying what it was *not*.

The cup from which He prayed to be delivered was not the cup of physical suffering. The cross was a mode of punishment invented by a cruel people, designed not only to inflict death, but to inflict it with the greatest degree of torture and indignity to the person to be crucified. It did not fail of its end. The sufferings of Christ on the cross were terrible, for He had a perfect body, as well as a true and reasonable soul. If it had been only His physical suffering of which He had been thinking, still Christ might have said, "Behold and see if there be any sorrow like to My sorrow, all you that pass by." But it was not the cup of mortal pain. If that were all, then Celsus and many a scoffer since, would be justified in contrasting the yielding, shrinking, agonizing conduct of Christ with that of many a soldier on the field of battle, criminal at the stake, or martyr in his last suffering for Christ.

Nor was it the cup of shame and obloquy. Christ was numbered with transgressors. The cross today surmounts the temples of our faith and is a symbol of all that is sacred and holy. But when Christ died upon the cross it was the "cursed tree." Rome would not permit one of her citizens to die on the cross, but Christ died on the cursed tree; and, as if to complete the shame of it, by accident or by design on the part of Pilate, Christ was crucified between two thieves. No drop in the cup of ignominy and shame was lacking. Yet this was not the cup from which Christ prayed to be delivered.

Nor was it the cup of human hatred and evil. Bitter indeed

was that cup, and more bitter to Christ than to any other, because greater was His perfect love for men. "Reproach hath broken my heart." Well might He say, "They hated Me without a cause." He came in the fullness of love to seek and to save men, but His own received Him not, and now over His head on the cross He sees breaking a fearful storm of hatred and execration such as the world had never seen. Well might the sun have hidden His face at the sight of men mocking and reviling Christ, if for no other reason. Yet this, I am sure, was not the cup from which He shrank.

Neither was it the impending treason of one disciple, the profane denial of another whom He had chosen and honored above all the rest, nor the cowardice and faithlessness of the others. One can take a blow from his enemies, but a blow from one's friends bows the head and breaks the heart. Christ is to drink that bitter cup and to know the blow, not of a stranger or an enemy, but of His own familiar friend with whom He had taken "sweet counsel together." But this, too, cannot have been the cup from which our Lord was shrinking.

The cup from which Christ prayed to be delivered was the cup of man's sin, mingled with his guilt and punishment. He was to taste death for every man, not physical death, but the death of the soul, the separation of the soul from God. The iniquity of us all was laid upon Him. He became our curse. He who knew no sin was made sin on our behalf. There you have the tragedy, the mystery, the beauty, and the power of Christ's suffering.

You say you do not understand that? Neither do I. Neither did the disciples. Who is asked to understand it? Even the angels do not understand, but desire to look into it. You are asked to believe it, to accept it, and to live by it.

If even Christ was amazed at the penalty He had to pay, if the angels themselves desire to look into it, then it will not be strange that we cannot fathom it with our own minds.

> But none of the ransomed ever knew
>   How deep were the waters crossed;
> Nor how dark was the night that the Lord passed through
>   Ere he found his sheep that was lost.

This last struggle with the tempter and with the temptation to draw back from the cross, like those which had preceded it in the desert and elsewhere, ended in a complete victory for Christ. The hardest battle of all was fought at the very foot of the cross, but the end of it was triumph and victory.

> This was compassion like a God,
> That when the Savior knew
> The price of pardon was his blood
> His pity ne'er withdrew.

Christ won this victory as He had won His other victories through complete reliance upon God's will. Even in His sorest agony, when He was praying that the cup might pass from Him, He always added, "Nevertheless, not my will, but thine, be done." Whatever God had spoken, whatever God had declared, He wished to be fulfilled in His life.

As He comes back from the field of His last battle to rouse the sleeping disciples and to face the traitor and the mob who had come to take Him, how calm, confident, majestic, Godlike is Jesus! The battle is over. To the winds and the waves which had agitated the deep sea of His soul Christ said in the fullness of His devotion to the will of God and in the depths of His love for lost sinners, "Peace, be still." Now behold Him, erstwhile the bleeding, agonizing struggler, as He awakens the slumbering disciples, or says to Judas, "Betrayest thou the Son of man with a kiss?" or confronts the angry mob who fall prostrate before Him, or, healing the servant's ear smitten by Peter, tells that disciple to put up his sword into its sheath, saying, "The cup which my Father hath given me, shall I not drink it?" and adding, "Thinkest thou that I cannot now pray to my Father, and he shall presently give me more than twelve legions of angels?"

Watch Him now as He goes bound in their midst, and yet King and Prince, to the judgment hall of Caiaphas, where Peter's sword will smite his Lord; and thence to Pilate and thence to Herod; thence back again to Pilate, and then to Golgotha and then up to the cross. How patient, how tender, how kinglike He is! What majestic sweetness now sits enthroned upon the Savior's brow! Now, eternal Son of God, bow Your head and die, and take with You into paradise the first fruits of Your passion, that poor, dying, penitent thief, who asked You to remember him in Your kingdom!

O lonely Sufferer! O solitary Agonizer! For me it was that You didst enter into Your agony. All Your disciples forsook You and fled; but You never forsake me or flee from me, unworthy though I am. Peter turned away from You, and with an oath denied that he ever knew You; but You did not turn away from him, and never will You turn away from me. Judas betrayed You with a kiss; but still you called him friend. He betrayed You, but never will You betray me nor put my soul to shame. Peter, James, and John all slept when You sweat the bloody sweat in Gethsemane; but You are the Savior who never slumbers nor sleeps. When I pass into Gethsemane, when I enter into my agony, when I go down into the river of Death, when I stand before the Judgment Seat, there, O Conqueror of Gethsemane and Calvary, I shall meet You, and I shall hear Your voice saying, "Come, ye blessed of my Father." "Enter thou into the joy of thy Lord." "Today shalt thou be with me in paradise."

So we come to the end of these sermons on Trials of Great Men of the Bible. Some of the men were tried by temptation to evil, some by the sunshine of power and prosperity, some by domestic sorrow and affliction, some by moral failure and breakdown. Yet all together enforce and illustrate the great truth that there is a Divinity at work in our lives and that the purpose of the trials of life is to evoke and awaken the good that is within us, to subdue the evil, to qualify us to serve the kingdom of God in our day and generation, and to make us fit at length for His fellowship in the life which is to come.

Every one of us is on trial. How is your trial proceeding? What is it discovering in you? What is it making out of you? It must end either in success or in failure. The victory will come only through watching and prayer, through battling and through faith, until at length

> . . . life's trial time shall end,
> And heavenly peace be won.